INFOGRAPHIC GUIDE TO CYCLING

RCUK
ROADCYCLINGUK

BLOOMSBURY
LONDON • NEW DELHI • NEW YORK • SYDNEY

contents

BICYCLE WHEELS

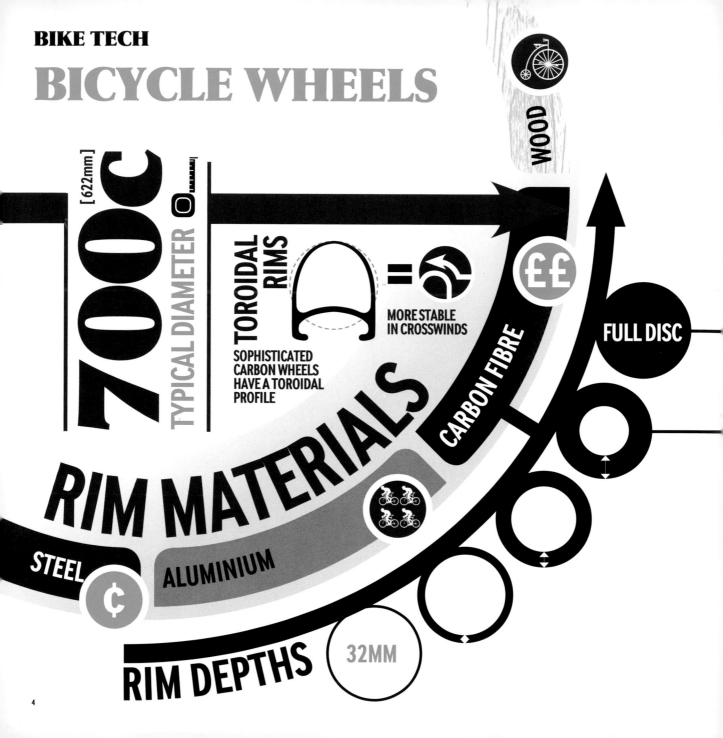

700c
[622mm]

TYPICAL DIAMETER

WOOD

TOROIDAL RIMS

= MORE STABLE IN CROSSWINDS

SOPHISTICATED CARBON WHEELS HAVE A TOROIDAL PROFILE

£££

FULL DISC

CARBON FIBRE

RIM MATERIALS

STEEL ¢ ALUMINIUM

RIM DEPTHS 32MM

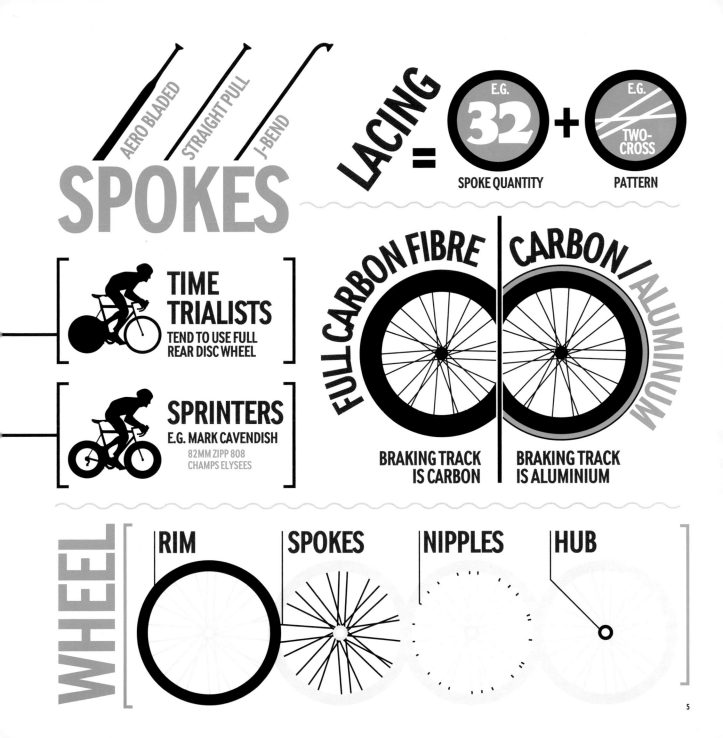

SPOKES

AERO BLADED · STRAIGHT PULL · J-BEND

LACING

=
E.G. 32 SPOKE QUANTITY
+
E.G. TWO-CROSS PATTERN

TIME TRIALISTS TEND TO USE FULL REAR DISC WHEEL

SPRINTERS E.G. MARK CAVENDISH
82MM ZIPP 808
CHAMPS ELYSEES

FULL CARBON FIBRE
BRAKING TRACK IS CARBON

CARBON / ALUMINIUM
BRAKING TRACK IS ALUMINIUM

WHEEL

RIM · **SPOKES** · **NIPPLES** · **HUB**

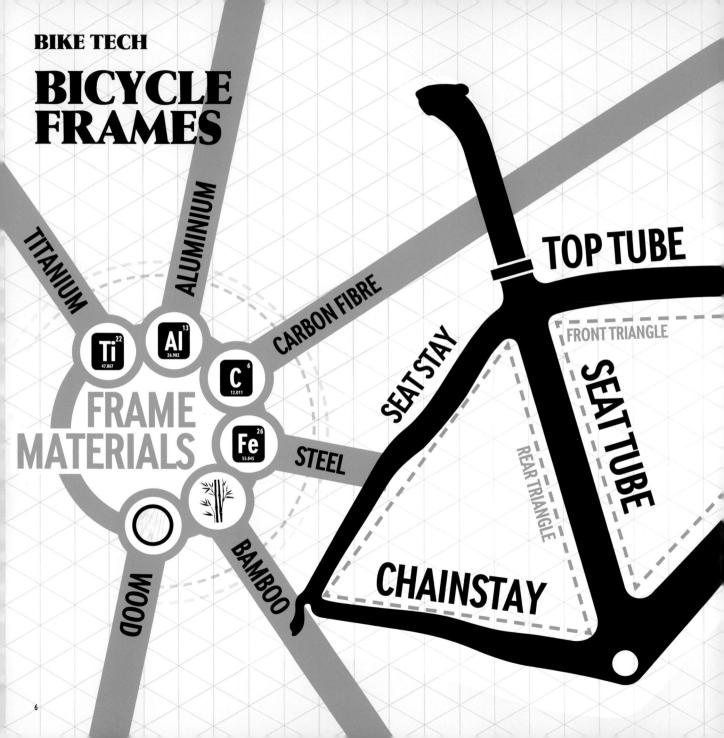

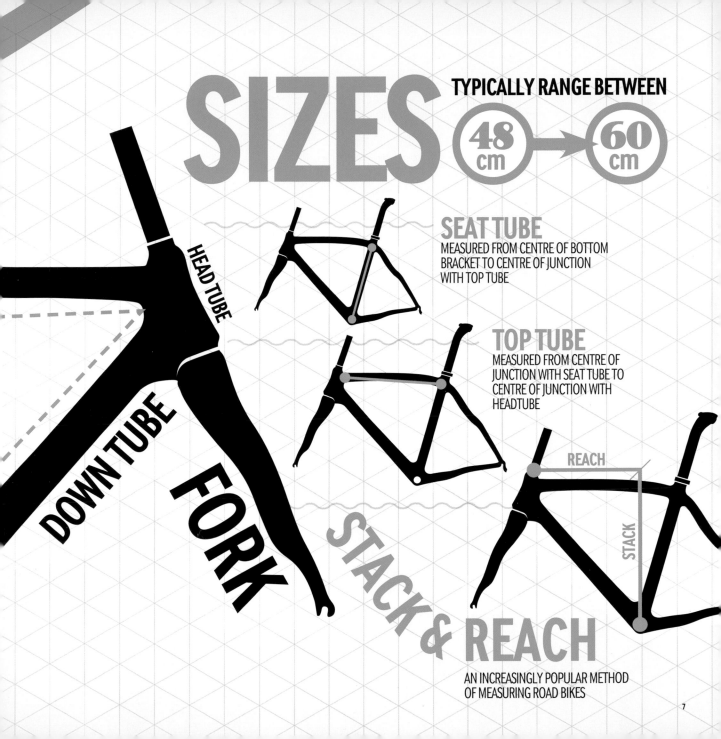

SIZES

TYPICALLY RANGE BETWEEN

48 cm ➔ **60 cm**

HEAD TUBE

DOWN TUBE

FORK

STACK & REACH

SEAT TUBE
MEASURED FROM CENTRE OF BOTTOM BRACKET TO CENTRE OF JUNCTION WITH TOP TUBE

TOP TUBE
MEASURED FROM CENTRE OF JUNCTION WITH SEAT TUBE TO CENTRE OF JUNCTION WITH HEADTUBE

REACH

STACK

AN INCREASINGLY POPULAR METHOD OF MEASURING ROAD BIKES

CARBON FRAME CONSTRUCTION
RESIN TRANSFER MOULDING (RTM) PROCESS

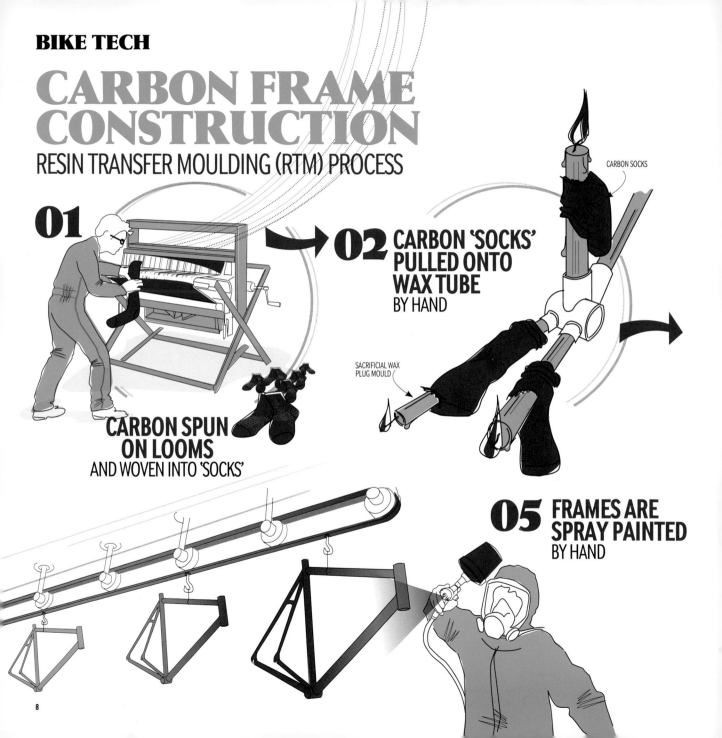

01 CARBON SPUN ON LOOMS
AND WOVEN INTO 'SOCKS'

02 CARBON 'SOCKS' PULLED ONTO WAX TUBE
BY HAND

CARBON SOCKS

SACRIFICIAL WAX PLUG MOULD

05 FRAMES ARE SPRAY PAINTED
BY HAND

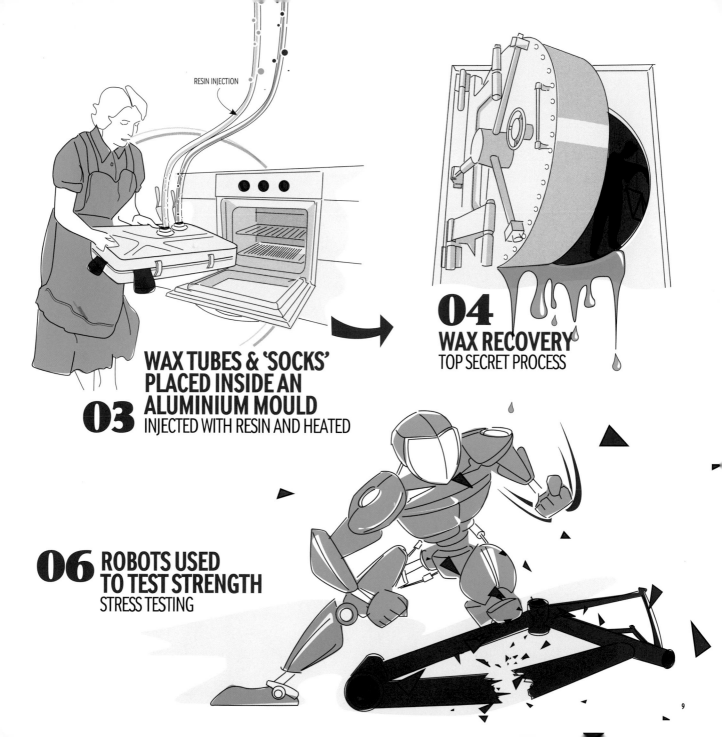

RESIN INJECTION

WAX TUBES & 'SOCKS' PLACED INSIDE AN 03 ALUMINIUM MOULD INJECTED WITH RESIN AND HEATED

04 WAX RECOVERY TOP SECRET PROCESS

06 ROBOTS USED TO TEST STRENGTH STRESS TESTING

9

DRIVETRAIN COMPONENTS

CASSETTE
A COLLECTION OF SPROCKETS

TYPICAL RATIOS

11-23 TEETH

11-25 TEETH

12-28 TEETH

MADE FROM
STEEL

Fe 26
55.845

+

C 6
12.011

JOCKEY WHEEL

CONTROLLED BY
RIGHT SHIFTER

JOCKEY WHEEL

INVENTED BY
TULIO CAMPAGNOLO

REAR DERAILLEUR
GUIDES THE CHAIN UP AND DOWN THE CASSETTE

MOVEMENT CONTROL BY
ELECTRONIC

OR

MECHANICAL

MICROCHIP/ ELECTRIC MOTOR

CABLE TENSION FROM LEVER

MOUNTED ON THE HANDLEBARS

SHIFTERS
TYPICALLY CONTAINED IN THE SAME UNIT AS THE BRAKE LEVER

MECHANICAL SHIFTERS CONTAIN A

RATCHET MECHANISM
WHICH PULLS A STEEL CABLE IN DEFINED INCREMENTS
'INDEXED SHIFTING'

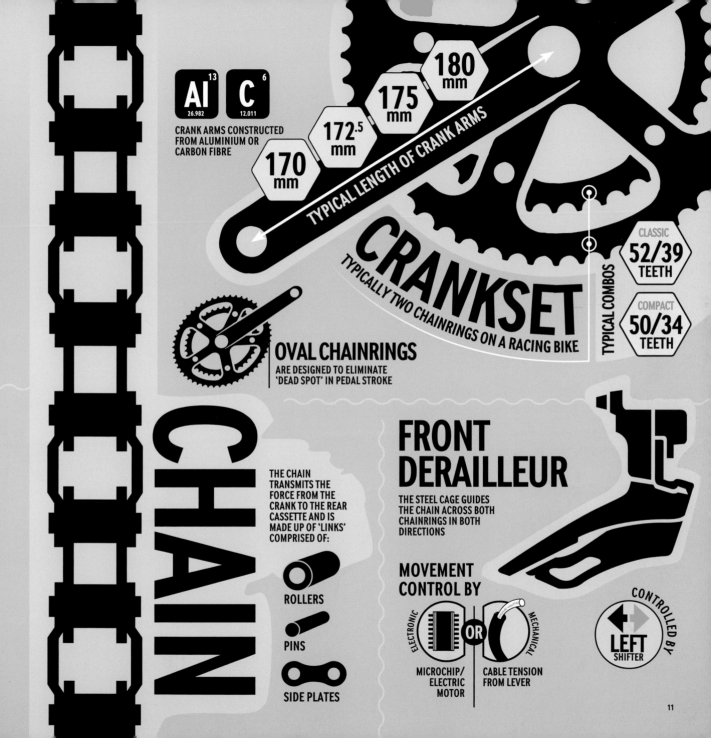

Al 13 — 26.982 **C** 6 — 12.011

CRANK ARMS CONSTRUCTED FROM ALUMINIUM OR CARBON FIBRE

170 mm

172.5 mm

175 mm

180 mm

TYPICAL LENGTH OF CRANK ARMS

CRANKSET

TYPICALLY TWO CHAINRINGS ON A RACING BIKE

TYPICAL COMBOS

CLASSIC
52/39 TEETH

COMPACT
50/34 TEETH

OVAL CHAINRINGS
ARE DESIGNED TO ELIMINATE 'DEAD SPOT' IN PEDAL STROKE

CHAIN

THE CHAIN TRANSMITS THE FORCE FROM THE CRANK TO THE REAR CASSETTE AND IS MADE UP OF 'LINKS' COMPRISED OF:

ROLLERS

PINS

SIDE PLATES

FRONT DERAILLEUR

THE STEEL CAGE GUIDES THE CHAIN ACROSS BOTH CHAINRINGS IN BOTH DIRECTIONS

MOVEMENT CONTROL BY

ELECTRONIC **OR** MECHANICAL

MICROCHIP/ ELECTRIC MOTOR

CABLE TENSION FROM LEVER

CONTROLLED BY

LEFT SHIFTER

CHRIS KING R45 ROAD HUB

45 TEETH ON EACH PLATE

BEARINGS...
AND BEARING RACES ARE MANUFACTURED IN-HOUSE FROM LOCALLY SOURCED STEEL

HELICAL SPLINES
PUSH DRIVE RING AND DRIVEN RING TOGETHER WHEN FORCE IS APPLIED TO THE DRIVETRAIN THROUGH THE PEDALS...

NO SLIPPAGE
THANKS TO TIGHTER ENGAGEMENT FROM THE UNIQUE HELICAL SPLINE DESIGN, EVEN WHEN SUBJECTED TO SIGNIFICANT FORCE

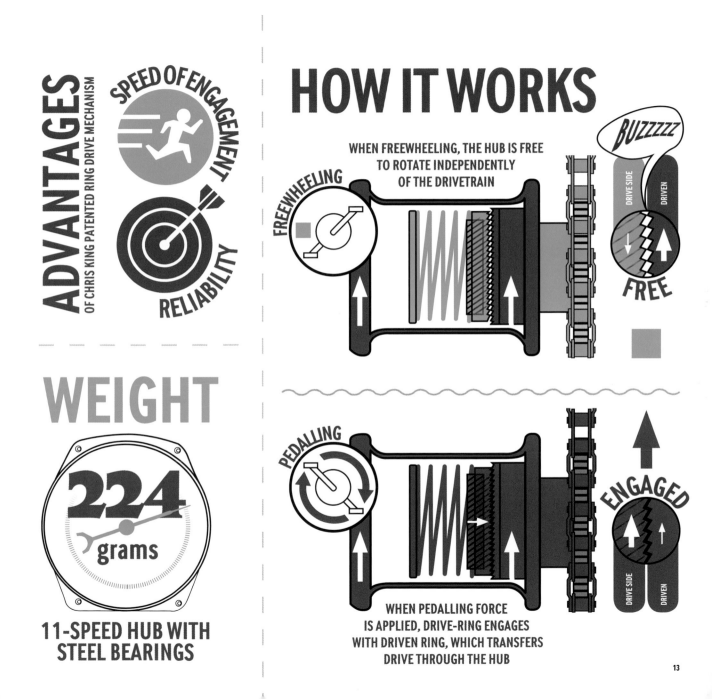

PROGRAMMABLE GEAR SHIFTING
SHIMANO Di2 PROJECT E-TUBE

INSIDE THE DERAILLEUR & FRONT MECH
CHIP AND MOTOR

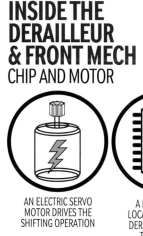

AN ELECTRIC SERVO MOTOR DRIVES THE SHIFTING OPERATION

A MEMORY CHIP LOCATED INSIDE THE DERAILLEUR STORES THE SETTINGS

LAPTOP TUNING SOFTWARE
HIGHLY CUSTOMISABLE

SHIFTERS CAN BE PROGRAMMED TO SHIFT UP OR DOWN, OR ONLY UP, OR ONLY DOWN! SABOTAGE A FRIEND'S BIKE

MULTIPLE SHIFTS
UP TO FOUR

THE DERAILLEUR CAN SHIFT UP TO FOUR GEARS IN ONE MOVEMENT

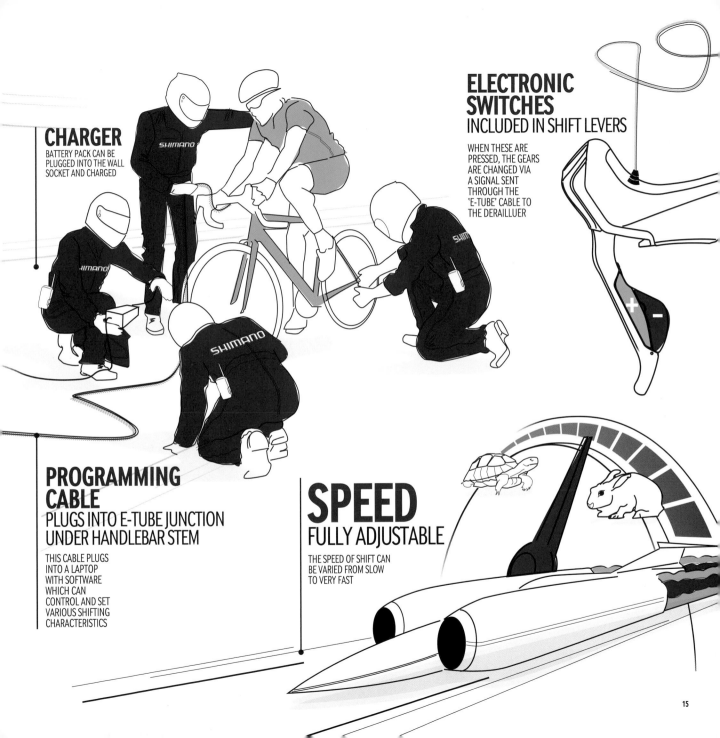

CHARGER

BATTERY PACK CAN BE
PLUGGED INTO THE WALL
SOCKET AND CHARGED

ELECTRONIC
SWITCHES
INCLUDED IN SHIFT LEVERS

WHEN THESE ARE
PRESSED, THE GEARS
ARE CHANGED VIA
A SIGNAL SENT
THROUGH THE
'E-TUBE' CABLE TO
THE DERAILLUER

PROGRAMMING
CABLE
PLUGS INTO E-TUBE JUNCTION
UNDER HANDLEBAR STEM

THIS CABLE PLUGS
INTO A LAPTOP
WITH SOFTWARE
WHICH CAN
CONTROL AND SET
VARIOUS SHIFTING
CHARACTERISTICS

SPEED
FULLY ADJUSTABLE

THE SPEED OF SHIFT CAN
BE VARIED FROM SLOW
TO VERY FAST

CLIPLESS PEDALS

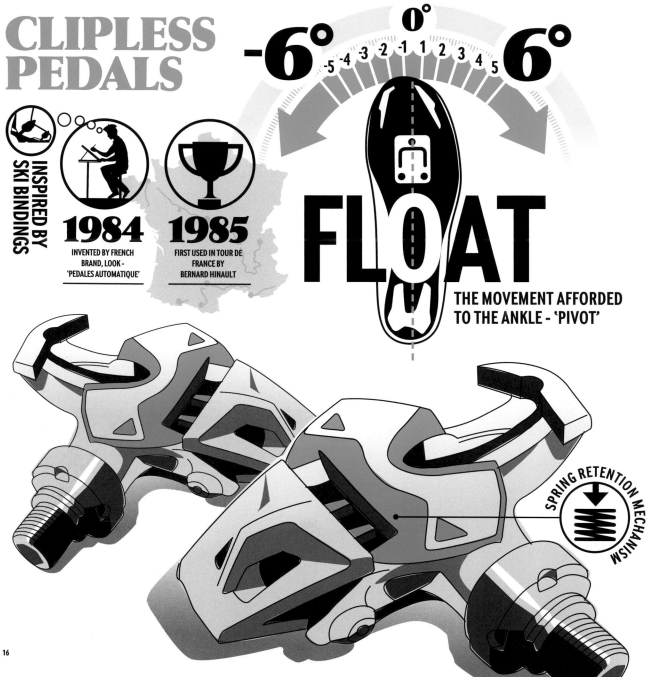

INSPIRED BY SKI BINDINGS

1984
INVENTED BY FRENCH BRAND, LOOK - 'PEDALES AUTOMATIQUE'

1985
FIRST USED IN TOUR DE FRANCE BY BERNARD HINAULT

-6° 0° 6°
-5 -4 -3 -2 -1 1 2 3 4 5

FLOAT

THE MOVEMENT AFFORDED TO THE ANKLE - 'PIVOT'

SPRING RETENTION MECHANISM

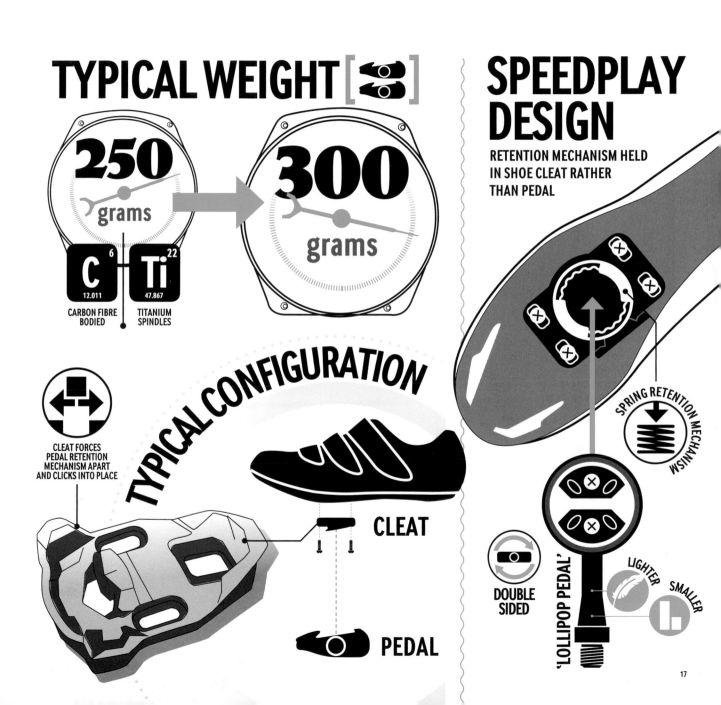

TYPICAL WEIGHT

250 grams

C 6 12.011
Ti 22 47.867

CARBON FIBRE BODIED

TITANIUM SPINDLES

300 grams

SPEEDPLAY DESIGN

RETENTION MECHANISM HELD IN SHOE CLEAT RATHER THAN PEDAL

TYPICAL CONFIGURATION

CLEAT FORCES PEDAL RETENTION MECHANISM APART AND CLICKS INTO PLACE

CLEAT

PEDAL

SPRING RETENTION MECHANISM

'LOLLIPOP PEDAL'

DOUBLE SIDED

LIGHTER

SMALLER

HYDRAULIC DISC BRAKES FOR ROAD BIKES

SHIMANO BR-R785 DISC BRAKE

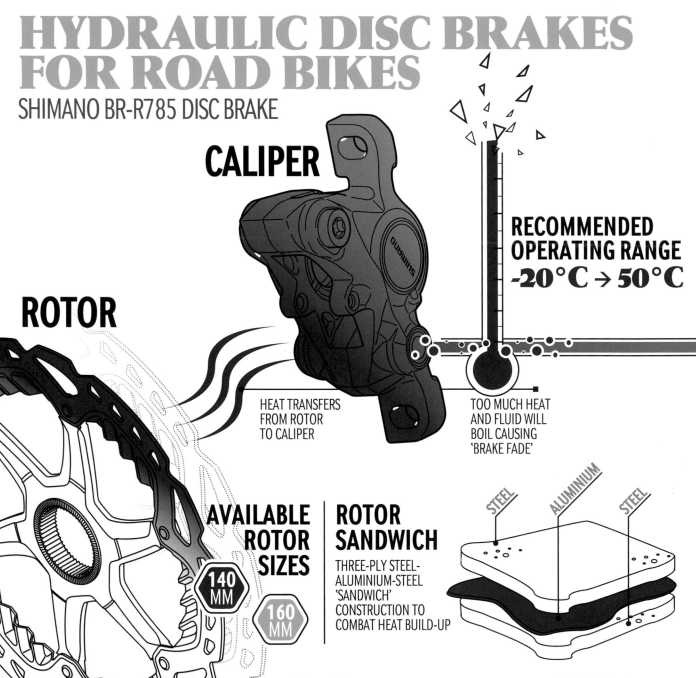

CALIPER

ROTOR

RECOMMENDED OPERATING RANGE -20°C → 50°C

HEAT TRANSFERS FROM ROTOR TO CALIPER

TOO MUCH HEAT AND FLUID WILL BOIL CAUSING 'BRAKE FADE'

AVAILABLE ROTOR SIZES

140 MM

160 MM

ROTOR SANDWICH

THREE-PLY STEEL-ALUMINIUM-STEEL 'SANDWICH' CONSTRUCTION TO COMBAT HEAT BUILD-UP

STEEL   ALUMINIUM   STEEL

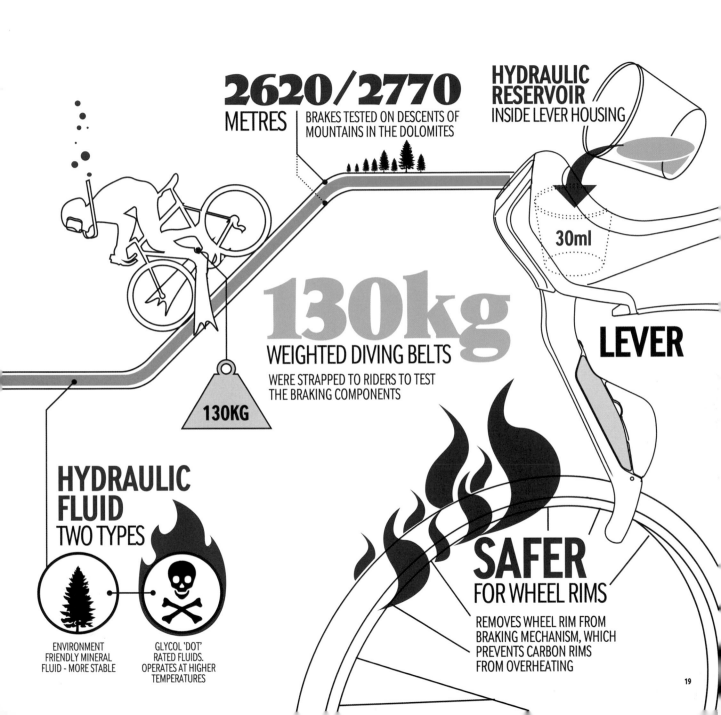

2620/2770 METRES BRAKES TESTED ON DESCENTS OF MOUNTAINS IN THE DOLOMITES

HYDRAULIC RESERVOIR INSIDE LEVER HOUSING

30ml

LEVER

130kg WEIGHTED DIVING BELTS WERE STRAPPED TO RIDERS TO TEST THE BRAKING COMPONENTS

130KG

HYDRAULIC FLUID TWO TYPES

ENVIRONMENT FRIENDLY MINERAL FLUID - MORE STABLE

GLYCOL 'DOT' RATED FLUIDS. OPERATES AT HIGHER TEMPERATURES

SAFER FOR WHEEL RIMS

REMOVES WHEEL RIM FROM BRAKING MECHANISM, WHICH PREVENTS CARBON RIMS FROM OVERHEATING

INSIDE A £9,000 PRO BIKE

DAVID MILLAR'S CERVELO S3

MINIMUM ALLOWABLE WEIGHT
FOR UCI COMPETITION

6.8 KG

CARBON FIBRE FRAME

STRONG & LIGHT

AUTO ADJUSTING FRONT MECH
SENSES CHAIN RUB AND ADJUSTS CLEARANCE TO PREVENT FRICTION

110

£2200
FRAME

30g

CARBON FIBRE BOTTLE CAGES
EXTREMELY LIGHTWEIGHT

880g

£1350
PEDALS

OVALIZED CRANKSET
TO ELIMINATE 'DEADSPOT'

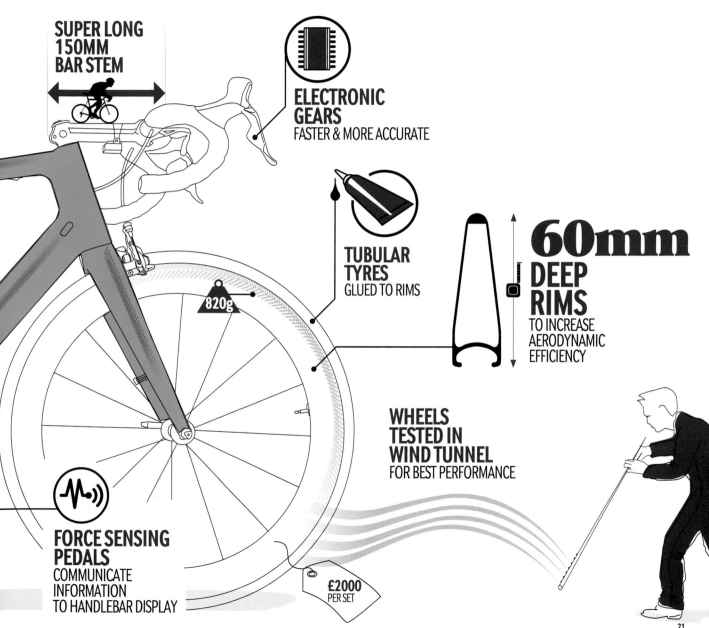

SUPER LONG 150MM BAR STEM

ELECTRONIC GEARS
FASTER & MORE ACCURATE

TUBULAR TYRES
GLUED TO RIMS

820g

60mm DEEP RIMS
TO INCREASE AERODYNAMIC EFFICIENCY

WHEELS TESTED IN WIND TUNNEL
FOR BEST PERFORMANCE

FORCE SENSING PEDALS
COMMUNICATE INFORMATION TO HANDLEBAR DISPLAY

£2000 PER SET

INSIDE A £16,000 PRO BIKE

BRADLEY WIGGINS' PINARELLO BOLIDE

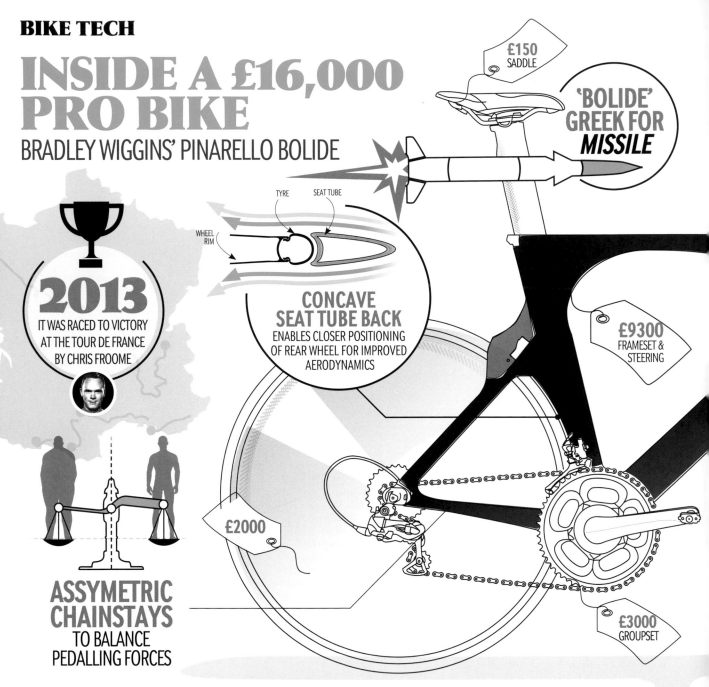

£150 SADDLE

'BOLIDE' GREEK FOR *MISSILE*

TYRE

SEAT TUBE

WHEEL RIM

CONCAVE SEAT TUBE BACK
ENABLES CLOSER POSITIONING OF REAR WHEEL FOR IMPROVED AERODYNAMICS

£9300 FRAMESET & STEERING

2013
IT WAS RACED TO VICTORY AT THE TOUR DE FRANCE BY CHRIS FROOME

£2000

£3000 GROUPSET

ASSYMETRIC CHAINSTAYS TO BALANCE PEDALLING FORCES

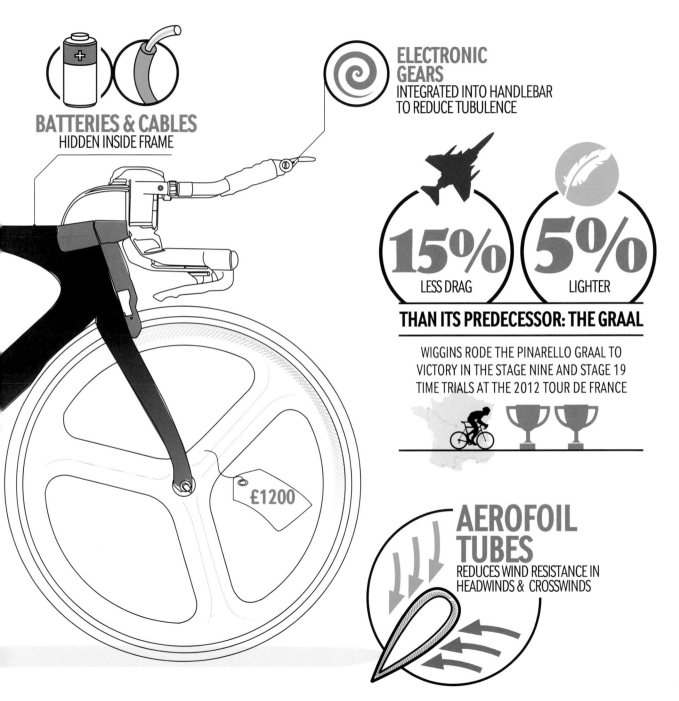

BATTERIES & CABLES
HIDDEN INSIDE FRAME

ELECTRONIC GEARS
INTEGRATED INTO HANDLEBAR
TO REDUCE TUBULENCE

15% LESS DRAG

5% LIGHTER

THAN ITS PREDECESSOR: THE GRAAL

WIGGINS RODE THE PINARELLO GRAAL TO
VICTORY IN THE STAGE NINE AND STAGE 19
TIME TRIALS AT THE 2012 TOUR DE FRANCE

£1200

AEROFOIL TUBES
REDUCES WIND RESISTANCE IN
HEADWINDS & CROSSWINDS

ANATOMY OF A TRACK BIKE

DROPOUT
SECTION OF FRAME THAT HOLDS THE REAR WHEEL AXLE

'SLIDING' DROPOUT: POSITION OF REAR WHEEL AFFECTS CHAIN TENSION

FRAME CONSTRUCTION

Fe 26	/	Al 13	/	C 6
55.845		26.982		12.011
STEEL		ALUMINIUM		CARBON MONOCOQUE

SINGLE CHAINWHEEL

FIXED GEAR
ONE SPROCKET

SPROCKET IS FIXED
REAR WHEEL TURNS CRANK

RIDER CANNOT FREEWHEEL

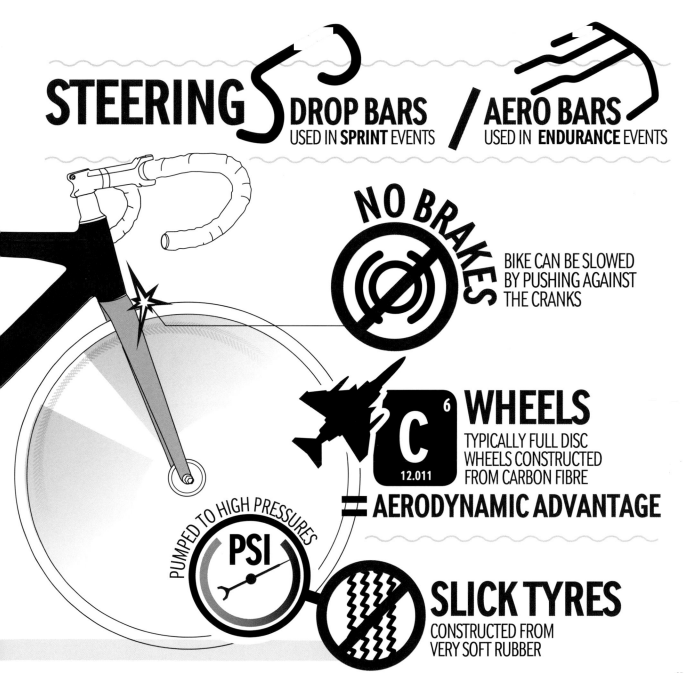

STEERING

DROP BARS USED IN **SPRINT** EVENTS / **AERO BARS** USED IN **ENDURANCE** EVENTS

NO BRAKES BIKE CAN BE SLOWED BY PUSHING AGAINST THE CRANKS

C 6 12.011 **WHEELS** TYPICALLY FULL DISC WHEELS CONSTRUCTED FROM CARBON FIBRE

= **AERODYNAMIC ADVANTAGE**

PUMPED TO HIGH PRESSURES PSI

SLICK TYRES CONSTRUCTED FROM VERY SOFT RUBBER

BIKE TECH
THREE STEPS TO A CLEAN BIKE

1 PREP

GLOVES SHAMPOO DEGREASER

2 CLEAN

BRUSH BUCKET SPONGE

3 DRY

AIRLINE TOWEL

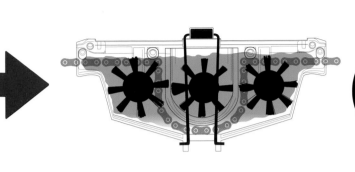

CHAIN BATH

JET WASH

CLEAN!

GRAND TOUR JERSEYS

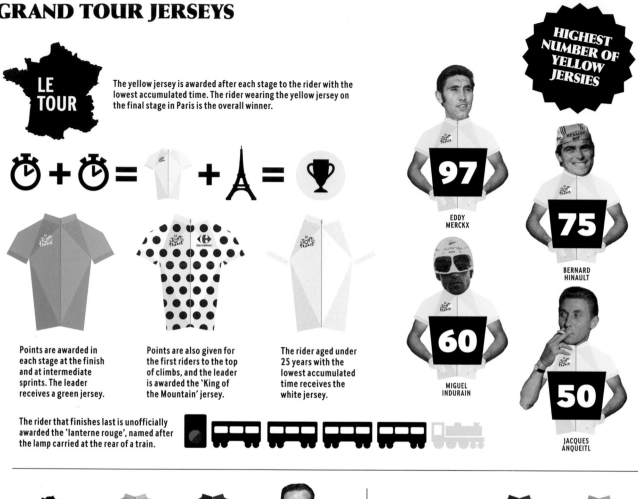

LE TOUR

The yellow jersey is awarded after each stage to the rider with the lowest accumulated time. The rider wearing the yellow jersey on the final stage in Paris is the overall winner.

Points are awarded in each stage at the finish and at intermediate sprints. The leader receives a green jersey.

Points are also given for the first riders to the top of climbs, and the leader is awarded the 'King of the Mountain' jersey.

The rider aged under 25 years with the lowest accumulated time receives the white jersey.

The rider that finishes last is unofficially awarded the 'lanterne rouge', named after the lamp carried at the rear of a train.

HIGHEST NUMBER OF YELLOW JERSIES

97 EDDY MERCKX

75 BERNARD HINAULT

60 MIGUEL INDURAIN

50 JACQUES ANQUEITL

LE GIRO

The 'maglia rosa' is worn by the overall time leader, the red by the points leader, blue by the mountain points leader, and the white by the leading rider under 25 years of age.

The 'maglia nera' given to the lowest placed rider was last awarded in 1952 to Giovanni Pinarello. He used the money to found the Pinarello bicycle company that currently supply Team Sky.

LA VUELTA

The red jersey is worn by the overall time leader, the green by the points leader, blue spots by the mountain points leader, and the white by the rider leading in all three catagories combined.

'LE MAILLOT JAUNE'

**The greatest prize in
professional cycling**

PHIL LIGGETT

1987 TOUR DE FRANCE, LA PLAGNE

...who is that rider coming up behind?
Because that...
LOOKS LIKE ROCHE!

GRAND TOURS – 1986 TOUR DE FRANCE

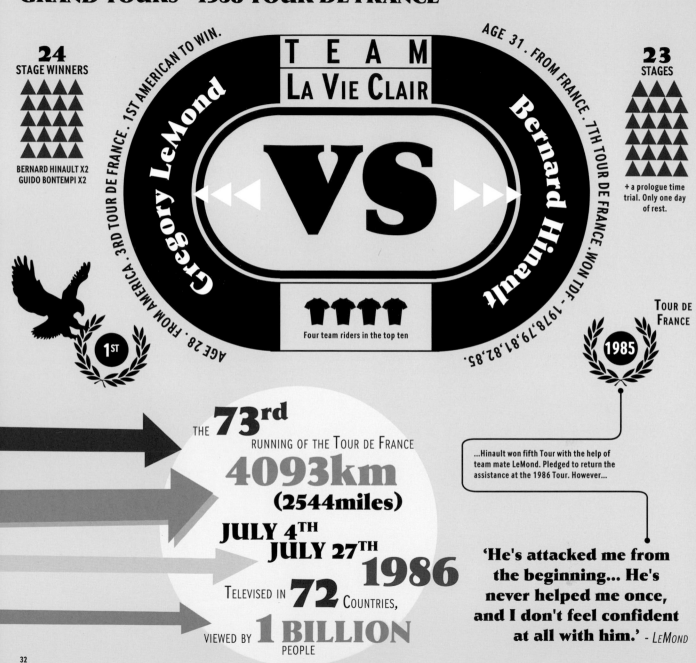

24
STAGE WINNERS

BERNARD HINAULT X2
GUIDO BONTEMPI X2

23
STAGES

+ a prologue time trial. Only one day of rest.

TEAM
La Vie Clair

VS

Four team riders in the top ten

1ST AMERICAN TO WIN. · 3RD TOUR DE FRANCE · AGE 28 · FROM AMERICA.

Gregory LeMond

AGE 31 · FROM FRANCE · 7TH TOUR DE FRANCE · WON TDF – 1978, 79, 81, 82, 85.

Bernard Hinault

1ST

TOUR DE FRANCE

1985

THE **73**RD RUNNING OF THE TOUR DE FRANCE
4093km
(2544miles)

JULY 4TH
JULY 27TH
1986

TELEVISED IN **72** COUNTRIES,
VIEWED BY **1 BILLION** PEOPLE

...Hinault won fifth Tour with the help of team mate LeMond. Pledged to return the assistance at the 1986 Tour. However...

'He's attacked me from the beginning... He's never helped me once, and I don't feel confident at all with him.' - LeMond

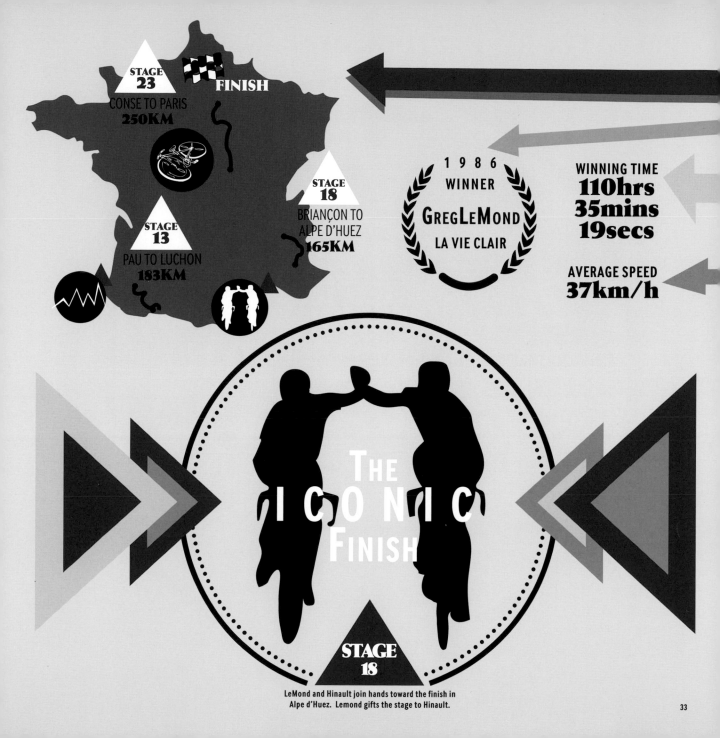

STAGE
23
CONSE TO PARIS
250KM

FINISH

STAGE
18
BRIANÇON TO
ALPE D'HUEZ
165KM

STAGE
13
PAU TO LUCHON
183KM

1986
WINNER
GregLeMond
LA VIE CLAIR

WINNING TIME
110hrs
35mins
19secs

AVERAGE SPEED
37km/h

THE
ICONIC
FINISH

STAGE
18

LeMond and Hinault join hands toward the finish in
Alpe d'Huez. Lemond gifts the stage to Hinault.

GRAND TOURS – 1987 TOUR DE FRANCE

26 STAGES

EIGHT YELLOW JERSEYS
Lech Piasecki (Poland)
First rider from 'Easten Bloc'
to lead Tour

VS

Stephen Roche AGE 27 FROM IRELAND TEAM CARRERA

Pedro Delgado AGE 27 FROM SPAIN TEAM PDM

74th EDITION

JULY 1ST >>>>>>> JULY 26

1987

CARRERA

207 RIDERS

23 TEAMS

23 STAGE WINNERS
JEAN-PAUL VAN POPPEL X2
JEAN-FRANÇOIS BERNARD X2

O² DEFICIT
Roche rides beyond his
limits to save his Tour
on La Plagne, 1987

GREG LEMOND
Defending champion absent
Accidentally shot while hunting turkeys

34

STAGE 15

Roche dropped on Alpe d'Huez
Delgado assumes yellow jersey

STAGE 18

Jean-Francois Bernard wins time
trial on the brutal Mont
Ventoux mountain

STAGE 19

Roche and Charly Mottet agree to
attack when Bernard is in the feed
zone. They pack extra supplies so
they don't have to stop.

STAGE 21

LE BOURGE D'OISANS
TO LA PLAGNE

Roche, Mottet and Pedro Delgado attack
on the descent of the Col du Galibier
(2655m) to drop Colombian rivals

The trio also drop Delgado's
team-mates so Roche attacks on the
following Col de la Madeleine

Delgado and team-mates regroup and
catch Roche on the stage-ending climb
of La Plagne

Roche, Mottet and Pedro Delgado attack
on the descent of the Col du Galibier
(2655m) to drop Colombian rivals

In the final part of the climb, Delgado
relaxes, believing Roche has blown

Roche attacks and almost catches Delgao
on the finish line Roche collapses,
prompting now legendary commentary:

STAGE 22

LA PLAGNE TO MORZINE
FINAL MOUNTAIN STAGE

39s between
Roche & Delgado

2 attacks by Delgado

Roche responds

Roche attacks

Delgado unable to respond

Roche
ends
stage **21**s

down on Delgado ahead of
penultimate stage time trial

1987

Roche wins world road
race championship
Second rider in history
(after Eddy Merckx)
to win cycling's Triple
Crown (Giro, Tour, and
Worlds in same year).

'Just who is that rider coming up behind because that looks like Roche!'
Phil Liggett

STAGE 24

DIJON INDIVIDUAL
TIME TRIAL
Roche finishes third. Nearly a
minute ahead of Delgado

STAGE 25

PARIS
Roche becomes first Irishman to
win the Tour de France

35

GRAND TOURS
2012 TOUR DE FRANCE
Sir Bradley Wiggins

D.O.B.
28.04.1980
HEIGHT
190cm
WEIGHT
69kg

'Kids from
Kilburn aren't
supposed to
win the Tour'
Wiggo

2013
KNIGHTHOOD
NEW YEAR'S
HONOURS

2013
OVERALL VICTORY
TOUR OF BRITAIN

2012
BBC SPORTS
PERSONALITY
OF THE YEAR

2012
OLYMPIC GOLD
MEDAL IN MEN'S
TIME TRIAL
LONDON

2012
TOUR DE FRANCE

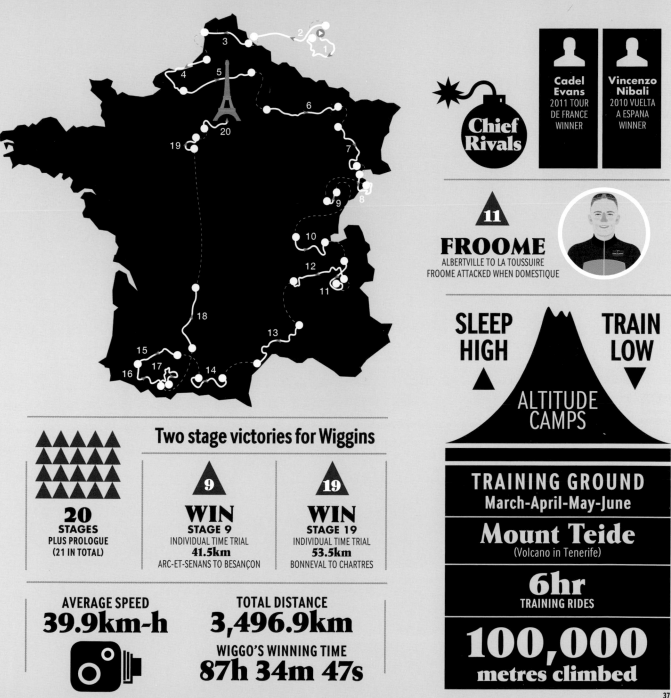

Chief Rivals

Cadel Evans
2011 TOUR DE FRANCE WINNER

Vincenzo Nibali
2010 VUELTA A ESPANA WINNER

11 FROOME
ALBERTVILLE TO LA TOUSSUIRE
FROOME ATTACKED WHEN DOMESTIQUE

SLEEP HIGH ▲   **TRAIN LOW** ▼

ALTITUDE CAMPS

TRAINING GROUND
March-April-May-June

Mount Teide
(Volcano in Tenerife)

6hr
TRAINING RIDES

100,000
metres climbed

Two stage victories for Wiggins

20 STAGES
PLUS PROLOGUE
(21 IN TOTAL)

9 WIN
STAGE 9
INDIVIDUAL TIME TRIAL
41.5km
ARC-ET-SENANS TO BESANÇON

19 WIN
STAGE 19
INDIVIDUAL TIME TRIAL
53.5km
BONNEVAL TO CHARTRES

AVERAGE SPEED
39.9km-h

TOTAL DISTANCE
3,496.9km

WIGGO'S WINNING TIME
87h 34m 47s

GRAND TOURS
2013 TOUR DE FRANCE
Chris Froome

**Froome's stage victories
at the 2013 Tour de France**

DOB: 20.05.1985
HEIGHT: 186CM
WEIGHT: 69KG
BORN: NAIROBI, KENYA
EARLY TRAINING GROUND:
RURAL HIGHLANDS OF NORTH NAIROBI

EARLY CAREER: RACED ON
KENYAN LICENCE, INCLUDING
2008 U-23 WORLD CHAMPS
LATER CAREER: HAS RACED ON
BRITISH LICENCE, SINCE 2008

'He has a VO2 max close
to the limits of known
physiological science.'
Frédéric Grappe, physiologist,
L'Equipe, July 2013

WINNING TIME
86hrs
56mins
40secs

8
WIN
STAGE 8
MOUNTAIN STAGE
195km
CASTRES TO AX3 DOMAINES

15
WIN
STAGE 15
MOUNTAIN STAGE
242.5km
GIVORS TO MONT VENTOUX

17
WIN
STAGE 17
MOUNTAIN TIME TRIAL
32km
EMBRUN TO CHRORGES

MICHELLE COUND

Girlfriend & vociferous defender
of Froome on Twitter

'If you want loyalty, get a Froome dog'
Tweet after Froome forced to wait for Wiggins on
climb to La Toussuire, TDF 2012, stage 11

CAREER
HIGHLIGHTS

2013
Tour de France
Criterium du Dauphine
Criterium International
Tour De Romandie

2014
Tour de Romandie
Tour of Oman

'This is a beautiful country and it
hosts the biggest annual sporting
event on the planet. To win the
100th edition is an honour...
This is one yellow jersey that will
stand the test of time'
**TOUR DE FRANCE WINNER'S SPEECH,
PODIUM, PARIS, 2013**

MOST EMBARRASSING
CAREER MOMENT

Riding into a race official after
rolling down the start ramp at
the world under-23 time trial
championship in 2008

AVERAGE SPEED
40.5kmh

TOTAL DISTANCE **3,404km**

GRAND TOURS – 2014 TOUR DE FRANCE
Vincenzo Nibali aka The Shark

D.O.B. **14.11.1984**
HEIGHT **181cm**
WEIGHT **65kg**
FROM **Sicily, Italy**

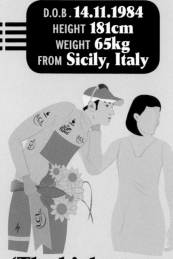

'The highest step
on the Champs-
Élysées podium...
It's more beautiful
than I ever imagined.'
Nibali

Chief Rivals

Chris Froome
CRASHES TWICE ON STAGE 5
AND IS OUT OF TOUR

Alberto Contador
CRASHES OUT STAGE 10

VICTORIES

2013
1ST OVERALL
GIRO D'ITALIA
STAGES 18 & 20

2013
1ST OVERALL GIRO
DEL TRENTINO

2013
1ST OVERALL
VUELTA A
ESPAGNA

le coq sportif

le TOUR de france

LCL
LE CRÉDIT LYONNAIS

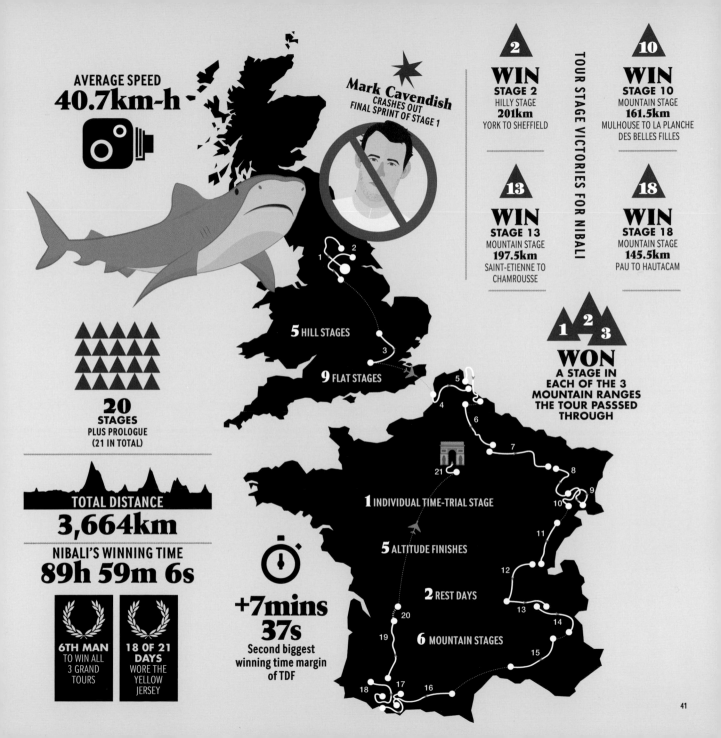

AVERAGE SPEED
40.7km-h

20
STAGES
PLUS PROLOGUE
(21 IN TOTAL)

TOTAL DISTANCE
3,664km

NIBALI'S WINNING TIME
89h 59m 6s

6TH MAN
TO WIN ALL
3 GRAND
TOURS

18 OF 21 DAYS
WORE THE
YELLOW
JERSEY

Mark Cavendish
CRASHES OUT
FINAL SPRINT OF STAGE 1

5 HILL STAGES

9 FLAT STAGES

TOUR STAGE VICTORIES FOR NIBALI

2
WIN
STAGE 2
HILLY STAGE
201km
YORK TO SHEFFIELD

10
WIN
STAGE 10
MOUNTAIN STAGE
161.5km
MULHOUSE TO LA PLANCHE
DES BELLES FILLES

13
WIN
STAGE 13
MOUNTAIN STAGE
197.5km
SAINT-ETIENNE TO
CHAMROUSSE

18
WIN
STAGE 18
MOUNTAIN STAGE
145.5km
PAU TO HAUTACAM

1 2 3
WON
A STAGE IN
EACH OF THE 3
MOUNTAIN RANGES
THE TOUR PASSSED
THROUGH

1 INDIVIDUAL TIME-TRIAL STAGE

5 ALTITUDE FINISHES

2 REST DAYS

6 MOUNTAIN STAGES

+7mins 37s
Second biggest
winning time margin
of TDF

41

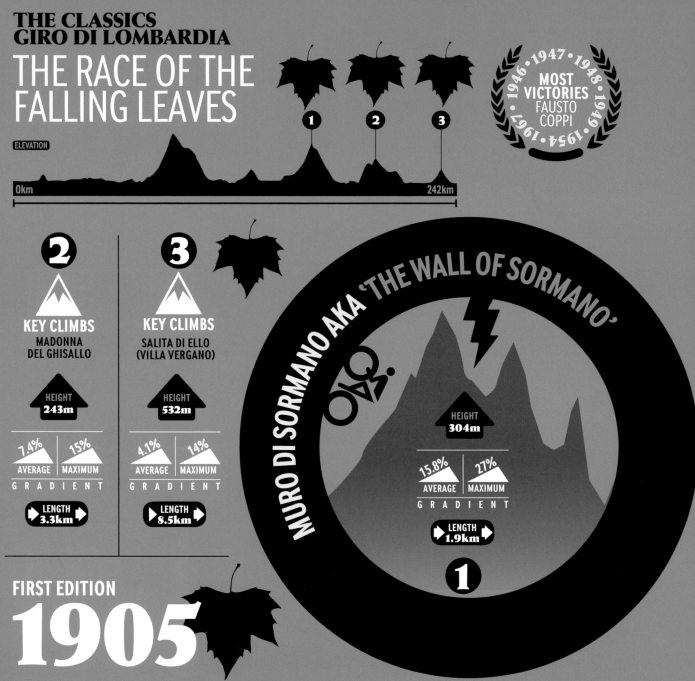

THE CLASSICS
GIRO DI LOMBARDIA

THE RACE OF THE FALLING LEAVES

MOST VICTORIES
FAUSTO COPPI
1946 · 1947 · 1948 · 1949 · 1954 · 1967

ELEVATION

0km   242km

2
KEY CLIMBS
MADONNA DEL GHISALLO

HEIGHT
243m

7.4% AVERAGE   15% MAXIMUM
G R A D I E N T

LENGTH
3.3km

3
KEY CLIMBS
SALITA DI ELLO (VILLA VERGANO)

HEIGHT
532m

4.1% AVERAGE   14% MAXIMUM
G R A D I E N T

LENGTH
8.5km

MURO DI SORMANO AKA 'THE WALL OF SORMANO'

HEIGHT
304m

15.8% AVERAGE   27% MAXIMUM
G R A D I E N T

LENGTH
1.9km

1

FIRST EDITION
1905

DISTANCE 242KM

2012 • 2013
TWO TIME CHAMPION
JOAQUIM RODRIGUEZ

LECCO

BERGAMO

43

THE CLASSICS
TOUR OF FLANDERS

De Ronde van Vlaanderen

'DE RONDE' ONE-DAY RACE IN SPRING
One of five 'Monuments' of the cycling calendar

1913
FIRST HELD

98
EDITIONS TO 2014

259
2014 LENGTH

12.9%
PATERBERG
DISTANCE: 360m

4.2%
KWAREMONT
DISTANCE: 2200m

6.6%
TAAIENBERG
DISTANCE: 530m

THOUSANDS OF FLANDERS FLAGS
ARE GIVEN OUT AT THE RACE.

FANS BRING GIANT
STANDARDS TO HANG OVER
THE FINISHING STRAIGHT

'HELLINGEN'
DE RONDE'S
SIGNATURE CLIMBS

11.6%
KOPPENBURG
DISTANCE: 600m

--THE COURSE--

Bruges

Oudenaarde

RECENT BRUGES TO MEERBEKE 2014: START BRUGES; END - OUDENAARDE

KINGS OF FLANDERS
68 Belgian victories from 98 winners

ACHIEL BUYSSE
1940+1941+1943

JOHAN MUSEEUW
('The Lion of Flanders')
1993+1995+1998

'TORANDO' TOM BOONEN
2005+2006+2012

45

MILAN
SAN REMO
LA PRIMAVERA
'THE CLASSIC OF SPRING'

START **Milano**

01

A
B
C

02

03

FINISH **SanRemo**

est
1907

105
EDITIONS

299km

TOTAL DISTANCE THE LONGEST CLASSIC

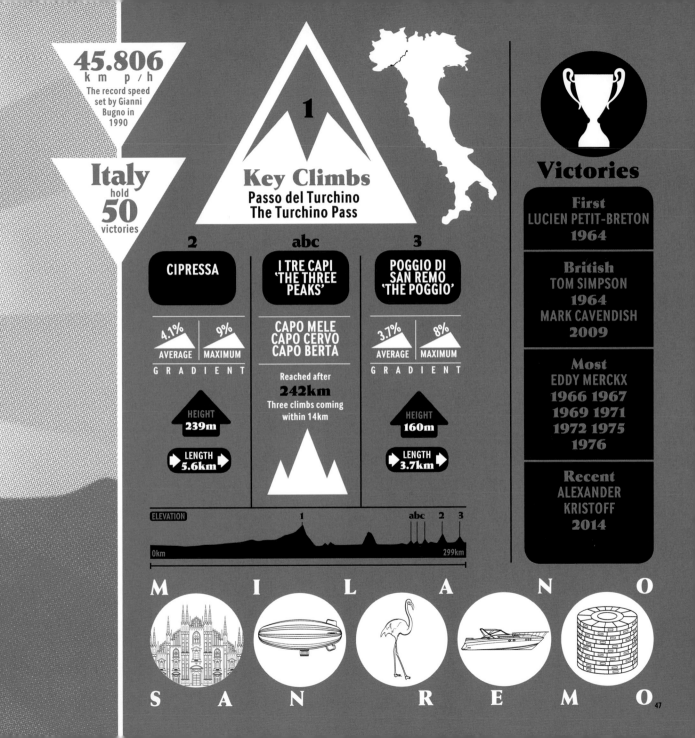

45.806 k m p / h
The record speed set by Gianni Bugno in 1990

Italy hold **50** victories

Key Climbs

1

Passo del Turchino
The Turchino Pass

2
CIPRESSA

GRADIENT
4.1% AVERAGE — 9% MAXIMUM

HEIGHT 239m

LENGTH 5.6km

abc
I TRE CAPI 'THE THREE PEAKS'

CAPO MELE
CAPO CERVO
CAPO BERTA

Reached after **242km**
Three climbs coming within 14km

3
POGGIO DI SAN REMO 'THE POGGIO'

GRADIENT
3.7% AVERAGE — 8% MAXIMUM

HEIGHT 160m

LENGTH 3.7km

ELEVATION
1   abc 2 3
0km   299km

Victories

First
LUCIEN PETIT-BRETON
1964

British
TOM SIMPSON
1964
MARK CAVENDISH
2009

Most
EDDY MERCKX
1966 1967
1969 1971
1972 1975
1976

Recent
ALEXANDER KRISTOFF
2014

M I L A N O
S A N R E M O

47

THE CLASSICS
LIEGE-BASTOGNE-LIEGE

One-day road race. One of five 'monuments' of the cycling calendar

SIGNATURE CLIMBS

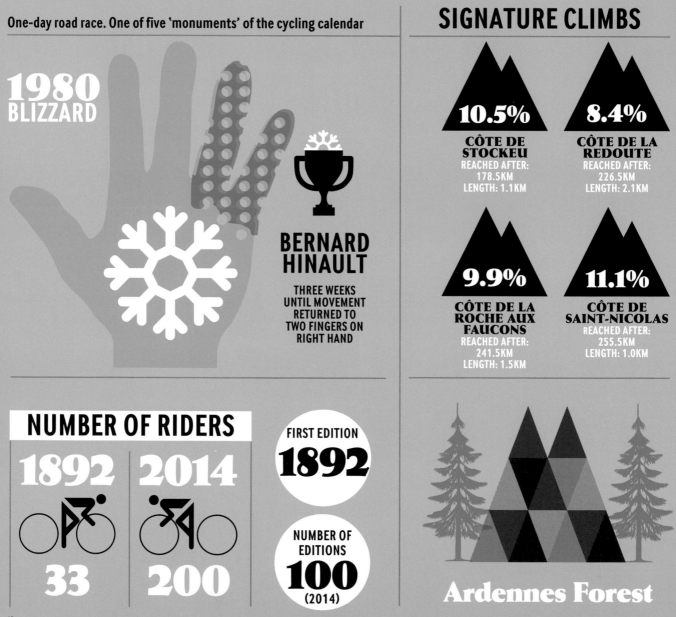

1980 BLIZZARD

BERNARD HINAULT

THREE WEEKS UNTIL MOVEMENT RETURNED TO TWO FINGERS ON RIGHT HAND

10.5%
CÔTE DE STOCKEU
REACHED AFTER:
178.5KM
LENGTH: 1.1KM

8.4%
CÔTE DE LA REDOUTE
REACHED AFTER:
226.5KM
LENGTH: 2.1KM

9.9%
CÔTE DE LA ROCHE AUX FAUCONS
REACHED AFTER:
241.5KM
LENGTH: 1.5KM

11.1%
CÔTE DE SAINT-NICOLAS
REACHED AFTER:
255.5KM
LENGTH: 1.0KM

NUMBER OF RIDERS

1892
33

2014
200

FIRST EDITION
1892

NUMBER OF EDITIONS
100
(2014)

Ardennes Forest

PHILIPPE
GILBERT
2011
ARDENNES
QUADRUPLE

FINISH ● ● START

2013
ROUTE WITH
MOUNTAIN STAGES

2013
WINNER
DANIEL MARTIN
CHASED TO FINISH LINE BY
MAN IN PANDA SUIT

THE CLASSICS PARIS-ROUBAIX

The Queen of the classics

STARTED:

1896

EDITIONS:

112

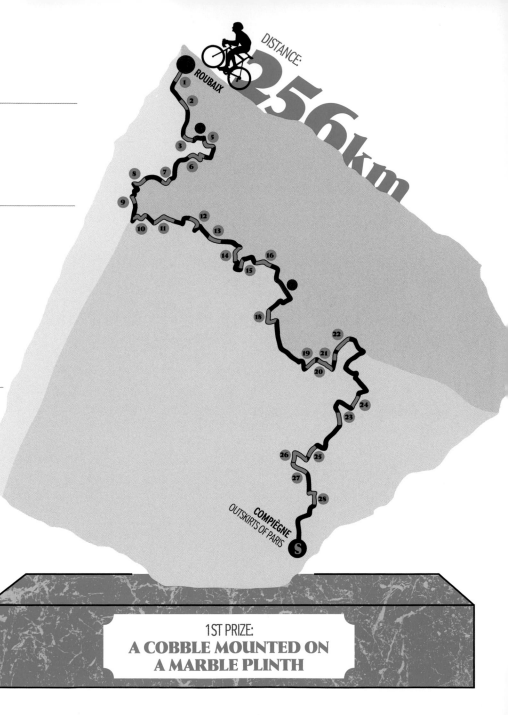

DISTANCE:

256km

ROUBAIX

COMPIÈGNE
OUTSKIRTS OF PARIS

MOST VICTORIES:

ROGER DE VLAEMINCK
BELGIUM
4 WINS

TOM BOONEN
BELGIUM
4 WINS

1ST PRIZE:
**A COBBLE MOUNTED ON
A MARBLE PLINTH**

28

★	2, 1
★★	24, 11, 9, 7, 3
★★★	27, 26, 23, 22, 21, 20, 19, 16, 15, 14, 13, 12, 8
★★★★	25, 18, 6, 5
★★★★★	17, 10, 4

17

TROUÉE D'ARENBERG
'THE TRENCH OF ARENBERG'
REACHED AFTER 161.5KM

WIN

4

LE CARREFOUR DE L'ARBRE
'THE CROSSROADS'
REACHED AFTER 240KM

**FREQUENTLY
DECISIVE**

DEAD STRAIGHT

2.4km

**FREQUENTLY
THE SCENE
OF TERRIBLE
CRASHES AS
BUNCH JOSTLES
FOR POSITION
TO HIT
COBBLES AT
TOP SPEED**

ROUBAIX VELODROME
RACE FINISH
REACHED AFTER 255KM

**VICTORY SHOWERS
REACHED AFTER 256KM**

1.5Laps
TO VICTORY

KINGS OF THE ROAD

Born
15.09.1919
Italy

Pro Teams

1939	Legnano
1942	
1945	S.S. Lazio Ciclismo/Bianchi
1946	Bianchi
1955	
1956	Carpano
1957	
1958	Bianchi
1959	Tricofilina

Il Campionissimo

'THE CHAMPION OF CHAMPIONS'

Rivals

GINO BARTALI
A RIVALRY THAT **DIVIDED ITALY**

COPPI
Hero of the progressve **North**

BARTALI
Hero of the religious and rural **South**

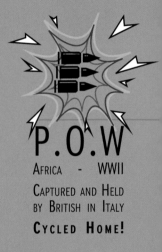

P.O.W
Africa – WWII
Captured and Held by British in Italy
Cycled Home!

Grand Tours & Career Wins

1942
WORLD HOUR RECORD
STOOD FOR **14 YEARS**

GIRO DI LOMBARDIA X5

GIRO D'ITALIA X5

MILAN-SAN REMO X3

WORLD CHAMPION 19 53

X2 TOUR DE FRANCE

PARIS - ROUBAIX LA FLECHE WALLONNE 19 50

Died
02.01.1960

Cause of Death:
UNKOWN

Malaria? Cocaine? Poison?

Hinted at use of performance Enhancing Drugs
WHILE STILL A RIDER

FAUSTO COPPI
'The Heron'

'MOST ACCOMPLISHED RIDER THAT CYCLING HAS EVER KNOWN' - *VÉLO*

BORN
17.06.1945
BELGIUM

PRO TEAMS

1965	SOLO-SUPERIA
1966 1967	PEUGEOT-BP-MICHELIN
1968 1970	FAEMA
1971 1976	MOLTENI
1977	FIAT
1978	C&A

RIVALS
MANY, MOSTLY...
BELGIAN

PUNCHED BY A SPECTATOR
1971

19 CLASSICS 'MONUMENT' VICTORIES

GRAND TOURS & CAREER WINS

GIRO D'ITALIA X5

TOUR DE FRANCE X5

X3 WORLD CHAMPIONSHIP

VUELTA A ESPANA 1973

HOUR RECORD
SET IN 1972 HELD FOR 12YRS

KINGS OF THE ROAD

'I RACE TO WIN, NOT TO PLEASE PEOPLE'

B O R N
26.01.1961
F R A N C E

L E P A T R O N

'RULER OF THE PELOTON'

HINAULT WAS WELL KNOWN FOR IMPOSING DISCIPLINE AND OFTEN COOPERATION AMONG RIDERS, ONCE FAMOUSLY DECREEING -

'THERE WILL BE **NO** ATTACKS TODAY BECAUSE TOMORROW'S STAGE WILL BE **DIFFICULT**'

GRAND TOURS &
CAREER WINS

2ND **1ST**

FINISHED
FIRST OR SECOND
IN EVERY TDF HE CONTESTED

MOST
SUCCESSFUL
FRENCH RIDER

PRO TEAMS

1975
1977 — GITANE-CAMPAGNOLO

1978
1983 — RENAULT-ELF-GITANE

1984
1986 — LA VIE CLAIRE

I N J U R Y

ABANDONED 1980 TOUR DE FRANCE DUE TO **KNEE INJURY**

CAME BACK LATER THAT YEAR **TO WIN WORLD ROAD RACE CHAMPIONSHIP**

TOUR DE FRANCE
X5

PARIS TO **1976** CAMEMBERT

VUELTA A ESPANA
.... **X2** ....

GIRO D'ITALIA
X3

1980
WORLD ROAD RACE CHAMPIONSHIPS
1979 1984
GIRO DI LOMBARDIA
1977 1978 1979 1982 1984
GRAND PRIX DES NATIONS
1981 **1977**
PARIS-ROUBAIX GHENT-WEVELGEM
1977 1980
LIEGE-BASTOGNE-LIEGE

BERNARD HINAULT
'The Badger'

GREG LEMOND
'The American'

THE SIGNATURE SPECS

BORN
12.08.1960
FRANCE

PROTEAMS

1982 RENAULT-ELF
1985

1986 SYSTEME U
1989

1990 CASTORAMA
1991

1992 GATORADE
1993

THESE WERE NOT THE
CAUSE OF THE NICKNAME

'LE PROFESSEUR'

HE WAS ONE OF FEW RIDERS
TO PASS HIS BACCALAUREAT

GRAND TOURS & CAREER WINS

MILAN - SAN REMO
1988
1989

GIRO D'ITALIA
1989

TOUR DE FRANCE
1983
1984

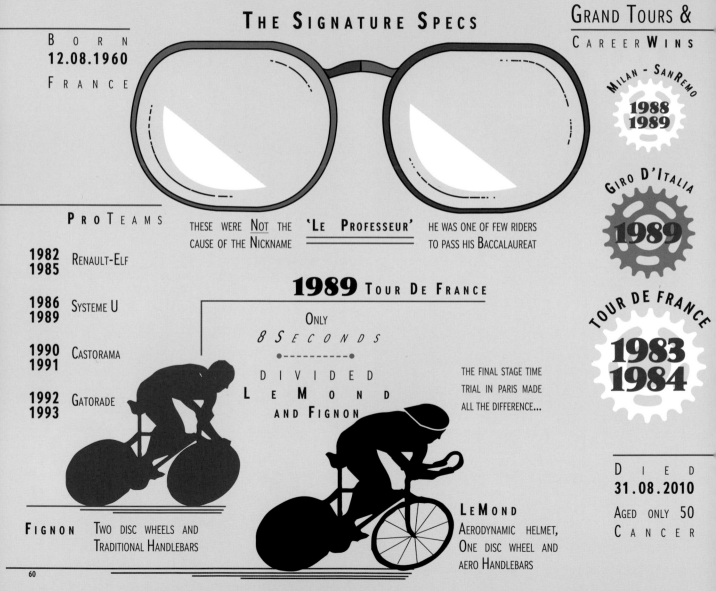

1989 TOUR DE FRANCE

ONLY
8 SECONDS
• - - - - - - - - - - - •
DIVIDED
LEMOND
AND FIGNON

THE FINAL STAGE TIME
TRIAL IN PARIS MADE
ALL THE DIFFERENCE...

FIGNON TWO DISC WHEELS AND
TRADITIONAL HANDLEBARS

LEMOND
AERODYNAMIC HELMET,
ONE DISC WHEEL AND
AERO HANDLEBARS

DIED
31.08.2010
AGED ONLY 50
CANCER

LAURENT FIGNON
'Le Professeur'

HOW ECHELONS SAVE CYCLISTS FROM CROSS WINDS

An echelon is a diagonal formation made by the riders in response to cross winds.

'In the gutter'

To be positioned on the extreme edge of an echelon, and left without shelter.

Omega Pharma-Quickstep team are the most effective in cross winds.

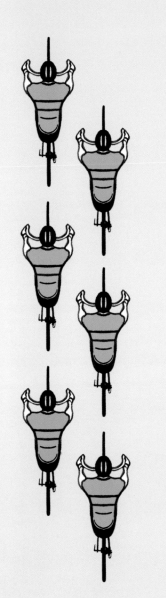

After taking a turn on the front, riders drop back through the echelon.

The rotation allows the workload to be shared and keeps the peloton moving with the greatest efficiency.

Cross winds split the peloton. Riding in the wind is much harder than riding in the shelter of other riders.

Riders scramble for a position in the echelon or risk being 'shelled' from the bunch, demanding a long and exhausting chase back on.

'When an echelon forms, it's like falling through ice – you've got five seconds or you are finished'

Mark Cavendish,
winner, stage 13,
Tour de France 2013

TACTICS – SPRINT TRAIN

Peloton

Teams fight for position to protect sprinter

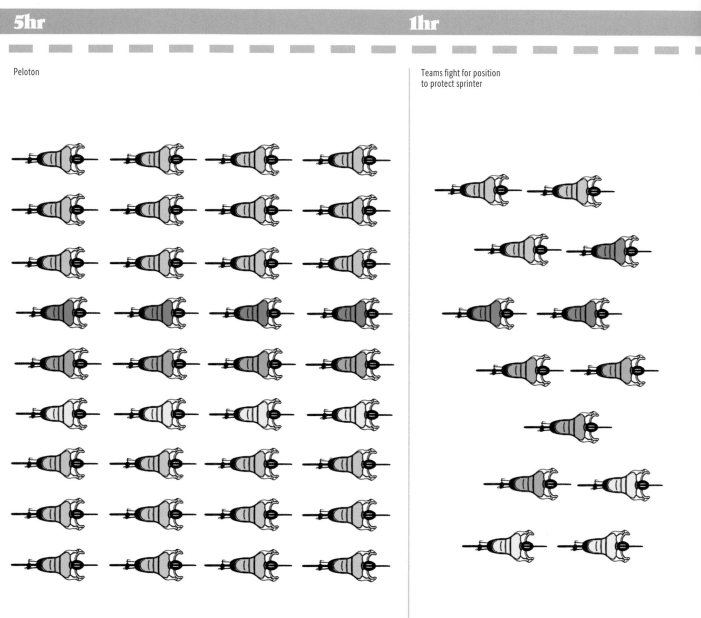

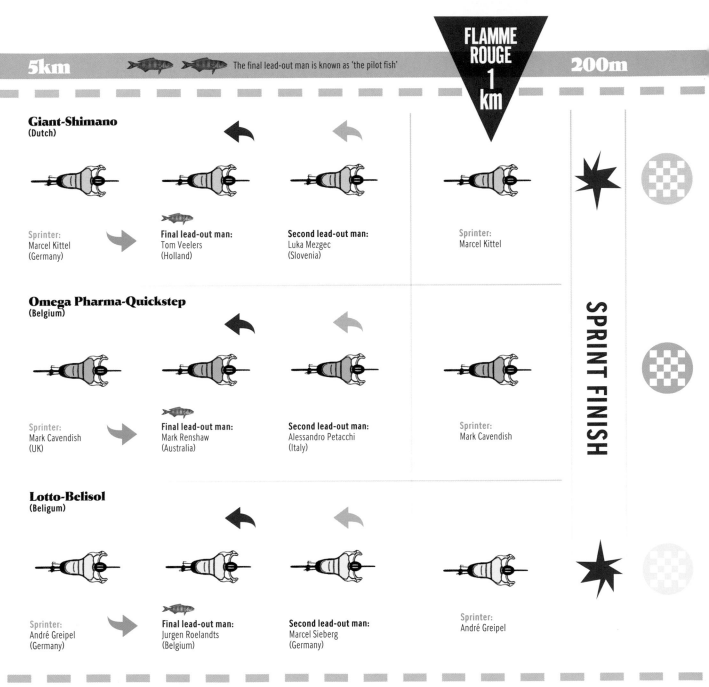

5km

The final lead-out man is known as 'the pilot fish'

FLAMME
ROUGE
1
km

200m

Giant-Shimano
(Dutch)

Sprinter:
Marcel Kittel
(Germany)

Final lead-out man:
Tom Veelers
(Holland)

Second lead-out man:
Luka Mezgec
(Slovenia)

Sprinter:
Marcel Kittel

Omega Pharma-Quickstep
(Belgium)

Sprinter:
Mark Cavendish
(UK)

Final lead-out man:
Mark Renshaw
(Australia)

Second lead-out man:
Alessandro Petacchi
(Italy)

Sprinter:
Mark Cavendish

Lotto-Belisol
(Beligum)

Sprinter:
André Greipel
(Germany)

Final lead-out man:
Jurgen Roelandts
(Belgium)

Second lead-out man:
Marcel Sieberg
(Germany)

Sprinter:
André Greipel

SPRINT FINISH

TACTICS – CLIMBING BREAKAWAY
Alberto Contador vs Chris Froome

Alberto Contador aka El Pistolero sprints.
Rivals are forced to catch him, he goes again.
Rivals, exhausted, can't respond. He thins out
the pursuing bunch with consecutive attacks,
until he is the last man standing.

EL PISTOLERO

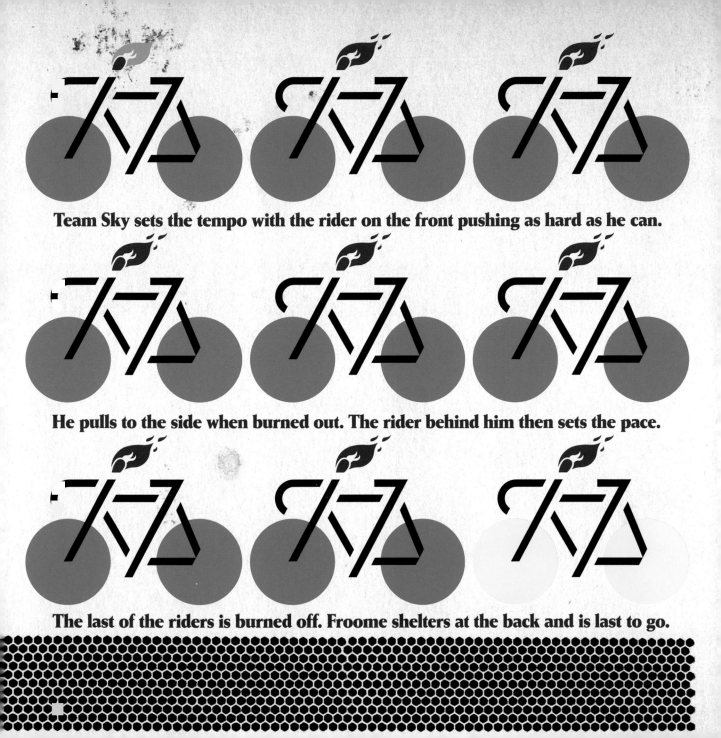

Team Sky sets the tempo with the rider on the front pushing as hard as he can.

He pulls to the side when burned out. The rider behind him then sets the pace.

The last of the riders is burned off. Froome shelters at the back and is last to go.

TACTICS – BREAKAWAY

Tour de France 2013: Stage 2 - Bastia to Ajaccio, Corsica.

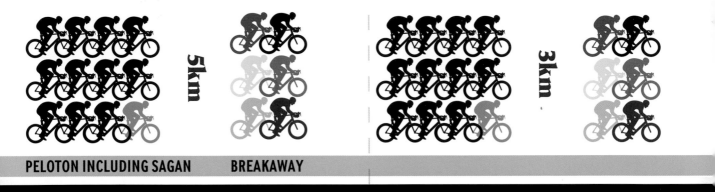

PELOTON INCLUDING SAGAN   **BREAKAWAY**

50KM P/H   **8 SECOND GAP**

Jan Bakelants in six-man escape group that rides clear with 5km of 156km stage remaining. Bakelants attacks with 2.5km remaining and clings on to win by a single second from a rampaging peloton led by green jersey winner, Peter Sagan. First victory of five-year professional career brings Bakelants the leader's yellow jersey in the biggest race in the world.

SAGAN   BAKELANTS

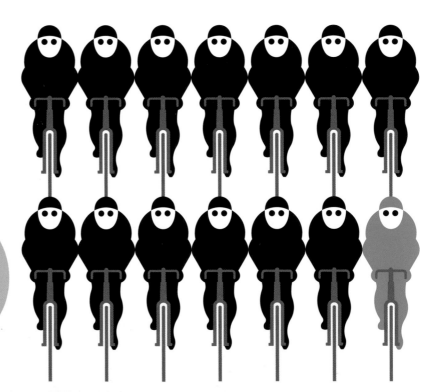

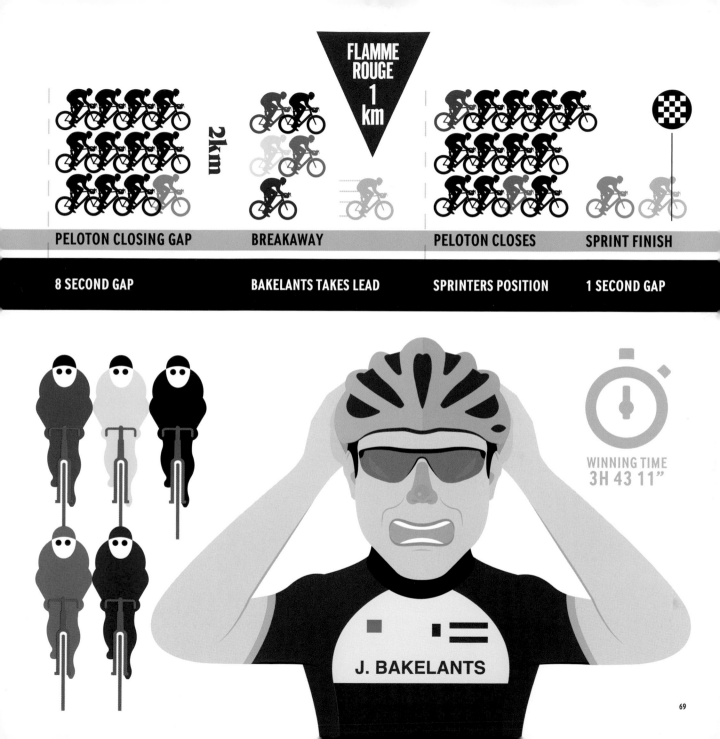

FLAMME ROUGE
1 km

2km

PELOTON CLOSING GAP   BREAKAWAY   PELOTON CLOSES   SPRINT FINISH

8 SECOND GAP   BAKELANTS TAKES LEAD   SPRINTERS POSITION   1 SECOND GAP

WINNING TIME
3H 43 11"

J. BAKELANTS

TACTICS – RIDING STYLES

SPRINT

WHEN — Finish line, intermediate sprints, escaping peloton

HOW — Out of saddle, hands on 'drops', weight over front of bike, pulling as well as pushing on pedals

WHO — Mark Cavendish

SEATED CLIMB

LONG CLIMBS **WHEN**

POSITIONED MID TO FRONT OF SADDLE, HANDS ON TOPS OF BARS **HOW**

WHO SIR BRADLEY WIGGINS

STANDING CLIMB

WHEN STEEP CLIMBS

HOW 'DANCING' ON PEDALS, HANDS ON LEVER HOODS

WHO ALBERTO CONTADOR

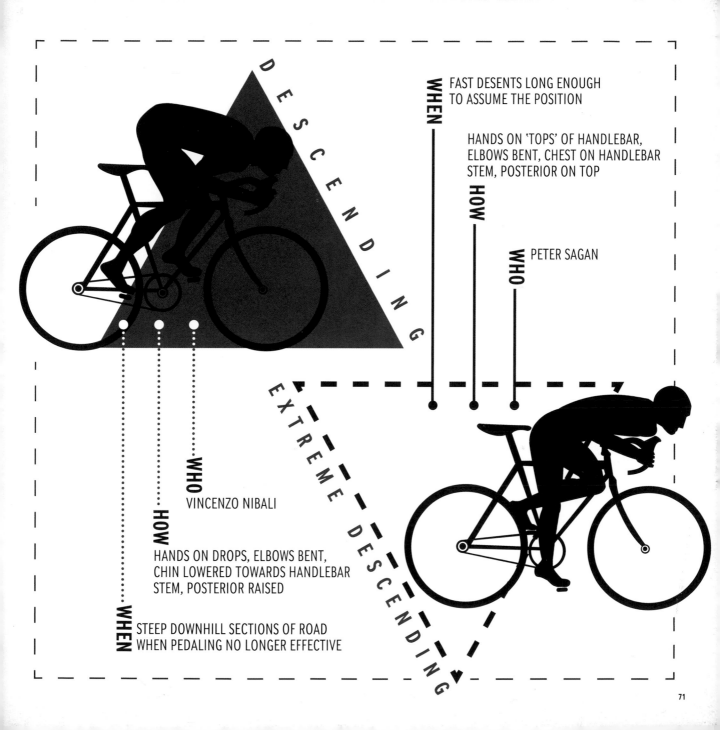

DESCENDING

WHEN FAST DESENTS LONG ENOUGH
TO ASSUME THE POSITION

HOW HANDS ON 'TOPS' OF HANDLEBAR,
ELBOWS BENT, CHEST ON HANDLEBAR
STEM, POSTERIOR ON TOP

WHO PETER SAGAN

EXTREME DESCENDING

WHO VINCENZO NIBALI

HOW HANDS ON DROPS, ELBOWS BENT,
CHIN LOWERED TOWARDS HANDLEBAR
STEM, POSTERIOR RAISED

WHEN STEEP DOWNHILL SECTIONS OF ROAD
WHEN PEDALING NO LONGER EFFECTIVE

BUILDING THE SUISSE VELODROME

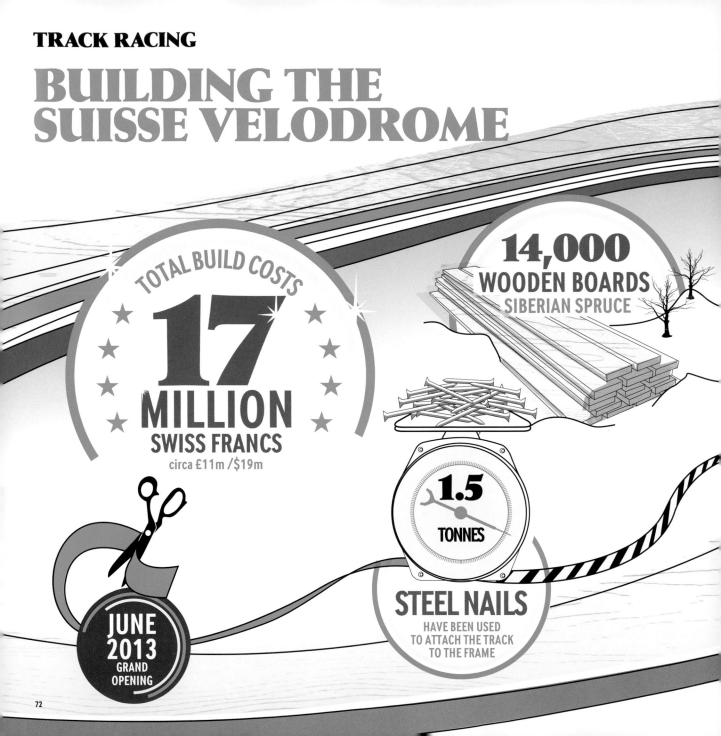

TOTAL BUILD COSTS

17 MILLION
SWISS FRANCS
circa £11m /$19m

JUNE 2013
GRAND OPENING

14,000
WOODEN BOARDS
SIBERIAN SPRUCE

1.5
TONNES

STEEL NAILS
HAVE BEEN USED TO ATTACH THE TRACK TO THE FRAME

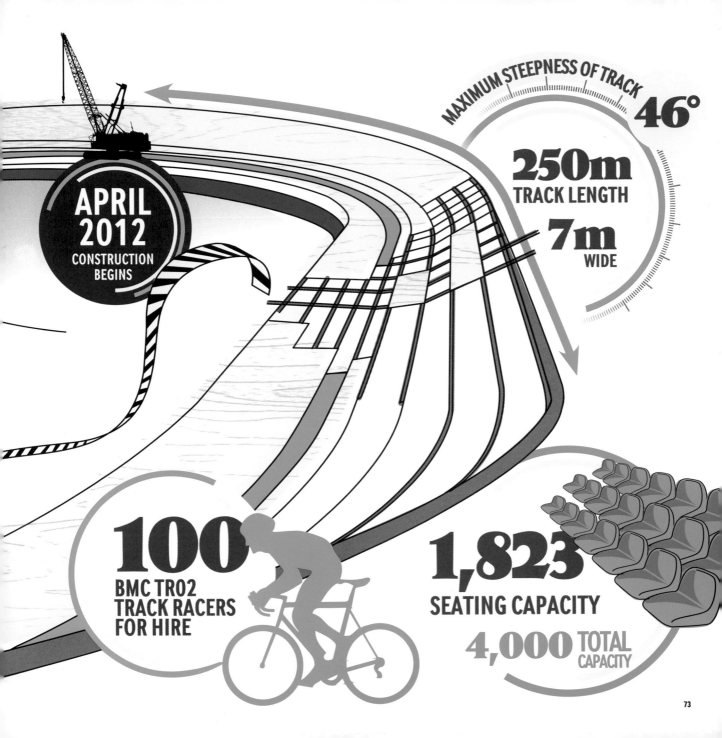

MAXIMUM STEEPNESS OF TRACK **46°**

250m TRACK LENGTH

7m WIDE

APRIL 2012 CONSTRUCTION BEGINS

100 BMC TR02 TRACK RACERS FOR HIRE

1,823 SEATING CAPACITY

4,000 TOTAL CAPACITY

TRACK RACING
Team Pursuit

GRAPHIC BASED ON TEAM GB WIN OVER AUSTRALIA
2012 OLYMPICS

START / FINISH LINE

4km
62kmh

EACH RACE HELD BETWEEN TWO TEAMS OF FOUR
TEAMS START ON OPPOSITE SIDE OF THE TRACK

OBJECTIVE IS TO CATCH THE OTHER TEAM
RIDERS TAKE TURNS TO LEAD THEIR TEAM-MATES

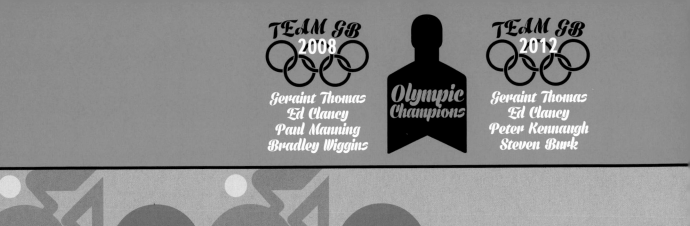

TEAM GB 2008
Geraint Thomas
Ed Clancy
Paul Manning
Bradley Wiggins

Olympic Champions

TEAM GB 2012
Geraint Thomas
Ed Clancy
Peter Kennaugh
Steven Burk

'The Australians have been blown away by sheer excellence'

THEY RIDE IN CLOSE FORMATION TO MAXIMISE AERODYNAMIC BENEFITS:
THE RIDER IN FRONT ACTS AS A WIND SHIELD FOR THE RIDER BEHIND

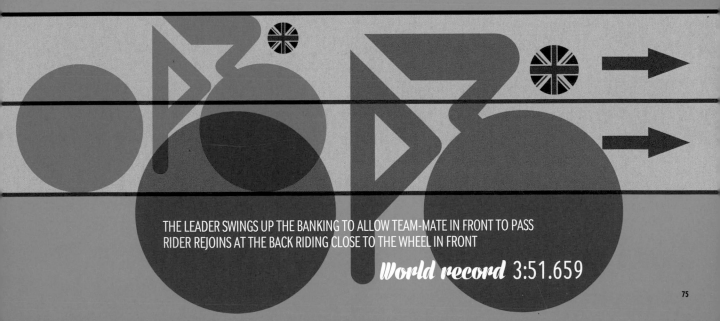

THE LEADER SWINGS UP THE BANKING TO ALLOW TEAM-MATE IN FRONT TO PASS
RIDER REJOINS AT THE BACK RIDING CLOSE TO THE WHEEL IN FRONT

World record 3:51.659

Individual Sprint
aka match sprint

Qualifying round is a one lap time trial

Elimination rounds follow until the final

Two riders start side-by-side and compete one-on-one

Early stages of race are highly tactical

Typically: race explodes and riders begin to sprint (sprint can begin at any time)

BELL RINGS FOR FINAL LAP

Forced into front   Attacks from behind

600m
OLYMPIC DISTANCE

GREAT BRITISH CHAMPIONS
Sir Chris Hoy

OLYMPIC CHAMPION
2008

WORLD CHAMPION
2008

Victoria Pendleton

OLYMPIC CHAMPION
2008

WORLD CHAMPION
**2005,2007
2008,2009
2010,2012**

TRACK RACING
Japanese Keirin

DERNY 98CC
MOTORISED BICYCLE

Zurcher two-stroke engine has a top speed of 50kmh

First bikes built by Roger Derny et Fils of Paris, in 1938

Pedalled by fixed gear with ratio>>>>>>>>>>>>>>>>>

FRONT CHAINRING 70t

REAR SPROCKET 11t

3-7 riders follow the Derny for the first 7 laps

Derny's speed gradually increases controlling the riders speed

Keirin is popular in Japan as a vehicle for gambling

Sprint Speeds:
Men 30kmh – 50kmh
Women 25kmh – 45kmh
Sprint after 600m – 700m

OLYMPIC CHAMPION 2008 2012 SIR CHRIS HOY

WORLD CHAMPION 2007 2008 2010 2012 SIR CHRIS HOY

GREAT BRITISH CHAMPIONS

OLYMPIC CHAMPION 2012 VICTORIA PENDLETON

WORLD CHAMPION 2007 VICTORIA PENDLETON

60 minutes to immortality

RECORD TYPES

Best Human Effort
Fewer technical restrictions

UCI Hour Record
Equipment restricted to similar standard to conventional track bike spoked wheels

The track is the most efficient surface and most easily measured for The Hour Record

1993 BORDEAUX
52.270 km
Chris Boardman
'Low profile Corima track bike'

1994 BORDEAUX
52.713 km
Graeme Obree
'Superman position'

RECORD BREAKERS

Longest distance in kilometres ridden
in a single hour on velodrome

1972 MEXICO CITY
49.431 km
Eddy Merckx
'Conventional bicycle with drop
handlebars and wire-spoked wheels'

1984 MEXICO CITY
51.151 km
Francesco Moser
'Low profile frameset with differently sized
wheels (700c/650c), and aero handlebars.'

1993 HAMAR, NORWAY
51.596 km
Graeme Obree
'Praying Mantis' position, courtesy of
homemade bicyle ('Old Faithful'),
built with washing machine bearings
in the bottom bracket

1996 MANCHESTER
56.375 km
Chris Boardman
'Superman position'

2000 MANCHESTER
49.441 km
Chris Boardman
'Conventional track bike'

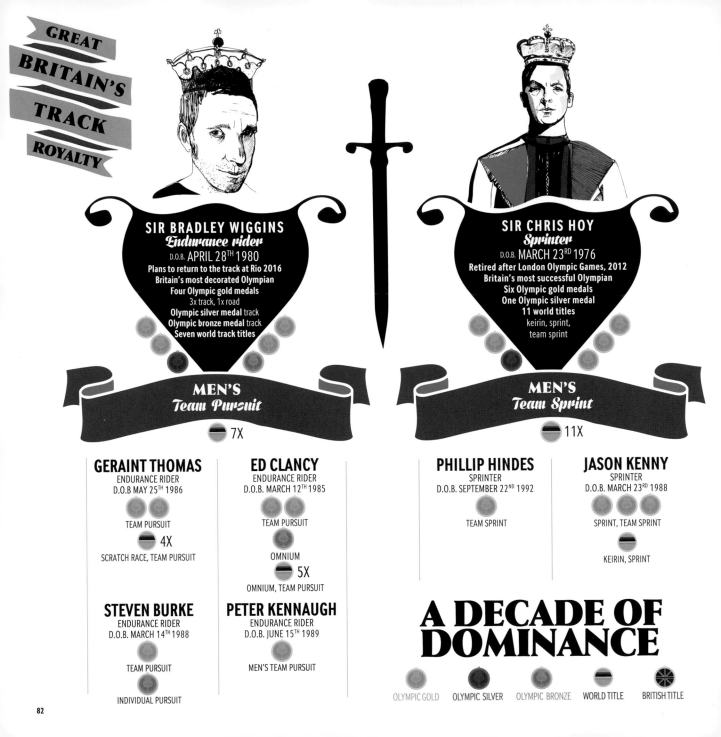

SIR BRADLEY WIGGINS
Endurance rider
D.O.B. APRIL 28TH 1980
Plans to return to the track at Rio 2016
Britain's most decorated Olympian
Four Olympic gold medals
3x track, 1x road
Olympic silver medal track
Olympic bronze medal track
Seven world track titles

SIR CHRIS HOY
Sprinter
D.O.B. MARCH 23RD 1976
Retired after London Olympic Games, 2012
Britain's most successful Olympian
Six Olympic gold medals
One Olympic silver medal
11 world titles
keirin, sprint,
team sprint

MEN'S
Team Pursuit
7X

MEN'S
Team Sprint
11X

GERAINT THOMAS
ENDURANCE RIDER
D.O.B MAY 25TH 1986
TEAM PURSUIT
4X
SCRATCH RACE, TEAM PURSUIT

ED CLANCY
ENDURANCE RIDER
D.O.B. MARCH 12TH 1985
TEAM PURSUIT
OMNIUM
5X
OMNIUM, TEAM PURSUIT

PHILLIP HINDES
SPRINTER
D.O.B. SEPTEMBER 22ND 1992
TEAM SPRINT

JASON KENNY
SPRINTER
D.O.B. MARCH 23RD 1988
SPRINT, TEAM SPRINT
KEIRIN, SPRINT

STEVEN BURKE
ENDURANCE RIDER
D.O.B. MARCH 14TH 1988
TEAM PURSUIT
INDIVIDUAL PURSUIT

PETER KENNAUGH
ENDURANCE RIDER
D.O.B. JUNE 15TH 1989
MEN'S TEAM PURSUIT

A DECADE OF DOMINANCE

OLYMPIC GOLD   OLYMPIC SILVER   OLYMPIC BRONZE   WORLD TITLE   BRITISH TITLE

VICTORIA PENDLETON
Sprinter
D.O.B. SEPTEMBER 24TH 1980
Retired after London Olympic Games 2012
Britain's most successful female Olympian
Two Olympic gold medals
women's keirin; women's sprint
Nine world titles
women's keirin, women's
sprint, women's
team sprint

WOMEN'S
Sprint
9X

LAURA TROTT
Endurance rider
D.O.B. APRIL 24TH 1992
Won first national title at age fourteen
Two Olympic gold medals
womens omnium; women's team pursuit
Five world titles
women's omnium,
team pursuit

WOMEN'S
Team Pursuit
5X

BECKY JAMES
SPRINTER
D.O.B. NOVEMBER 29TH 1991

WOMEN'S SPRINT,
WOMEN'S KEIRIN

JESS VARNISH
SPRINTER
D.O.B. NOVEMBER 19TH 1990

500M TT
TEAM SPRINT

WENDY HOUVENAGHEL
ENDURANCE RIDER
D.O.B. NOVEMBER 27TH 1974
**Retired after London
Olympic games, 2012**

WOMEN'S INDIVIDUAL PURSUIT

7X
WOMEN'S INDIVIDUAL AND TEAM PURSUIT

JOANNA ROWSELL
ENDURANCE RIDER
D.O.B. DECEMBER 5TH 1988

WOMEN'S TEAM PURSUIT
2X
WOMEN'S INDIVIDUAL PURSUIT,
WOMEN'S TEAM PURSUIT

DANI KING
ENDURANCE RIDER
D.O.B NOVEMBER 21ST 1990

WOMEN'S TEAM PURSUIT
3X
WOMEN'S TEAM PURSUIT

ELINOR BARKER
ENDURANCE RIDER
D.O.B. SEPTEMBER 7TH 1994

WOMEN'S TEAM PURSUIT
JUNIOR WOMEN'S ROAD TIME TRIAL

In the last 10 years, the Great Britain track cycling team has risen to the pinnacle of the sport. The team swept away the competition at the 2008 Beijing Olympic Games and became sporting superstars at London 2012, where tickets for the velodrome were the fastest to sell out. Their success has caused envy among rival nations, with the French repeating Sir Dave Brailsford's tongue-in-cheek remark that Team GB's wheels were especially round. The truth underlying their success is exceptional coaching, immensely gifted athletes, and the hard work of British Cycling's Secret Squirrel Club, the Chris Boardman-led team responsible for technical development.

UCI WORLDTOUR – TEAM JERSEYS

1 OMEGA PHARMA-QUICK STEP

2 MOVISTAR TEAM

3 TEAM KATUSHA

4 TEAM SKY

5 AG2R-LA MONDIALE

6 BMC RACING TEAM

7 TINKOFF-SAXO

8 TREK FACTORY RACING

9 ORICA-GREENEDGE

10
BELKIN PRO CYCLING TEAM

11
LAMPRE-MERIDA

12
GARMIN SHARP

13
TEAM GIANT-SHIMANO

14
CANNONDALE

15
ASTANA PRO TEAM

16
FDJ.FR

17
LOTTO BELISOL

18
TEAM EUROPCAR

UCI WORLDTOUR TEAMS
Global players: cycling's elite UCI WorldTour

3 KAZAKHSTAN
ASTANA PRO TEAM
Team manager: Alexander Vinokourov
Star rider: Vincenzo Nibali (Italy)
Bike: Specialized S-Works Tarmac

TINKOFF-SAXO
Team manager: Stefano Feltrin
Star rider: Alberto Contador
Bike: Specialized Roubaix, Specialized Tarmac, Specialized Venge

2 RUSSIA
TEAM KATUSHA
Team manager: Viatcheslav Ekimov
Star rider: Joaquim Rodríguez (Spain)
Bike: Canyon Ultimate CF SLX

1 UNITED STATES
BMC RACING TEAM
Team manager: Jim Ochowitz
Star rider: Cadel Evans
Bike: BMC Team Machine

GARMIN SHARP
Team manager: Jonathan Vaughters
Star rider: Daniel Martin
Bike: Cervelo S3, S5, R5

TREK FACTORY RACING
Team manager: Luca Guercilina
Star rider: Fabian Cancellara
Bike: Trek Madone 7, Trek Domane, Trek Emonda

5 BELGIUM
LOTTO BELISOL
Team manager: Bill Olivier
Star rider: André Greipel
Bike: Ridley Noah Fast

4 AUSTRALIA
ORICA-GREENEDGE
Team manager: Shayne Bannan
Star rider: Simon Gerrans
Bike: Scott Foil

OMEGA PHARMA-QUICK STEP
Team manager: Patrick Lefevere
Star rider: Tom Boonen, Mark Cavendish
Bike: Specialized Roubaix, Specialized Tarmac, Specialized Venge

6 FRANCE
AG2R-LA MONDIALE
Team manager: Vincent Lavenu
Star rider: Roman Bardet (France)
Bike: Focus Izalco Team SL Carbon

TEAM EUROPCAR
Team manager: Jene-René Bernaudeau
Star rider: Thomas Voeckler (France)
Bike: Colnago C59

FDJ.fr
Team manager: Marc Madiot
Star rider: Thibaut Pinot (France)
Bike: Lapierre Xelius EFI Ultimate

7 GREAT BRITAIN
TEAM SKY
Team manager: Sir David Brailsford
Star rider: Chris Froome
Bike: Pinarello Dogma 65.1 Think 2

8 NETHERLANDS
TEAM GIANT-SHIMANO
Team manager: Richard Plugge
Star rider: Robert Gesink (Netherlands)
Bike: Bianchi Oltre XR2

BELKIN
PRO CYCLING TEAM
Team manager: Richard Plugge
Star rider: Sep Vanmarcke
Bike: Bianchi Oltre XR2,
Bianchi Infinito CV

9 SPAIN
MOVISTAR TEAM
Team manager: Eusebio Unzué
Star rider: Nairo Quintana
Bike: Canyon Aeroad, Canyon
Ultimate, Canyon Speedmax

10 ITALY
CANNONDALE
Team manager: Roberto Amadio
Star rider: Peter Sagan
Bike: Cannondale SuperSix Evo

LAMPRE-MERIDA
Team manager: Giuseppe Saronni
Star rider: Rui Costa (Portugal)
Bike: Merida Reacto Evo

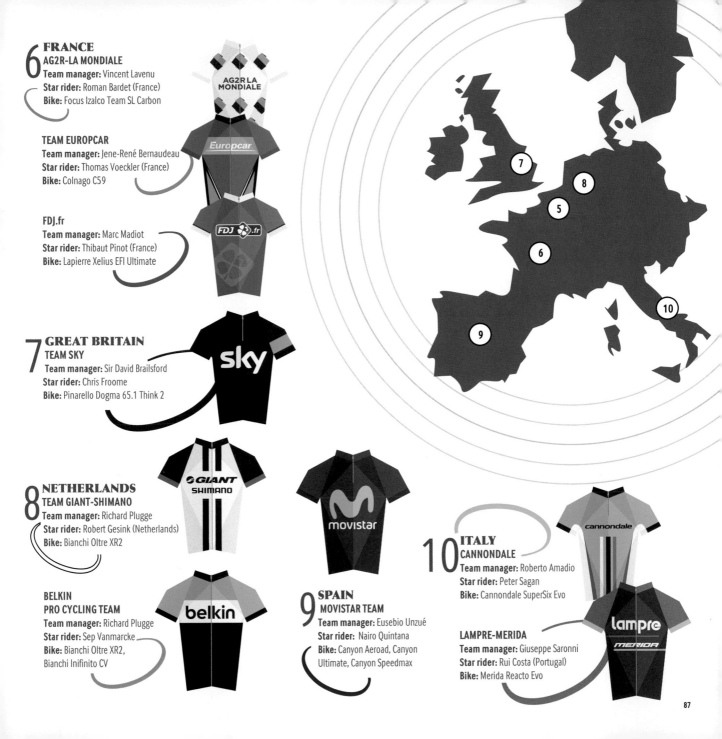

TEAM PERSONNEL – LOTTO BELISOL

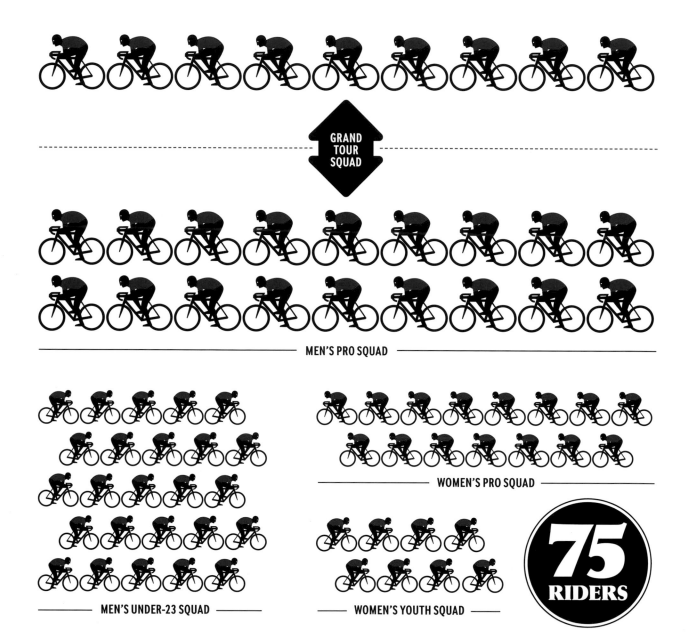

GRAND
TOUR
SQUAD

MEN'S PRO SQUAD

WOMEN'S PRO SQUAD

MEN'S UNDER-23 SQUAD

WOMEN'S YOUTH SQUAD

75 RIDERS

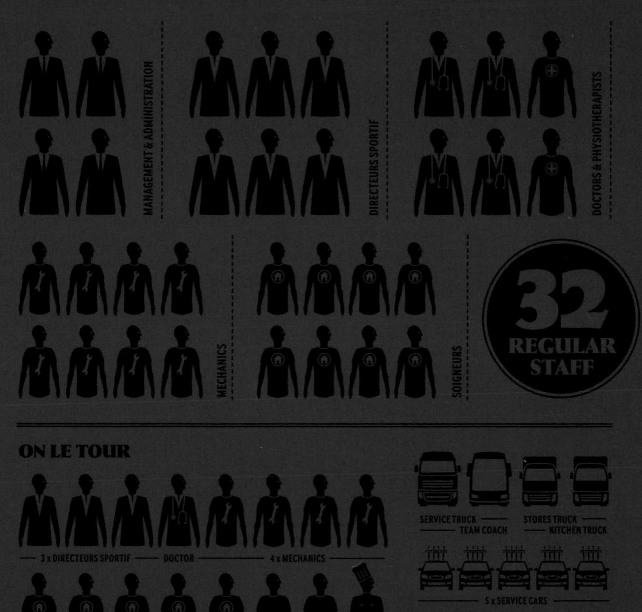

MANAGEMENT & ADMINISTRATION

DIRECTEURS SPORTIF

DOCTORS & PHYSIOTHERAPISTS

MECHANICS

SOIGNEURS

32 REGULAR STAFF

ON LE TOUR

— 3 x DIRECTEURS SPORTIF — DOCTOR — 4 x MECHANICS —

— 5 x SOIGNEURS — 2 x DRIVERS — CHEF —

SERVICE TRUCK — | TEAM COACH STORES TRUCK — | KITCHEN TRUCK

— 5 x SERVICE CARS —

— 5 x VIP CARS —

SERVICE TRUCKS – TEAM SKY

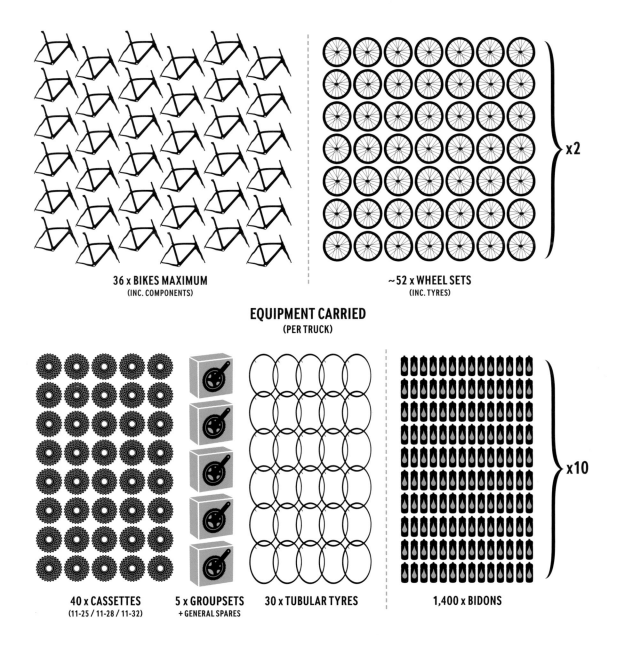

36 x BIKES MAXIMUM
(INC. COMPONENTS)

~52 x WHEEL SETS
(INC. TYRES)

x2

EQUIPMENT CARRIED
(PER TRUCK)

40 x CASSETTES
(11-25 / 11-28 / 11-32)

5 x GROUPSETS
+ GENERAL SPARES

30 x TUBULAR TYRES

1,400 x BIDONS

x10

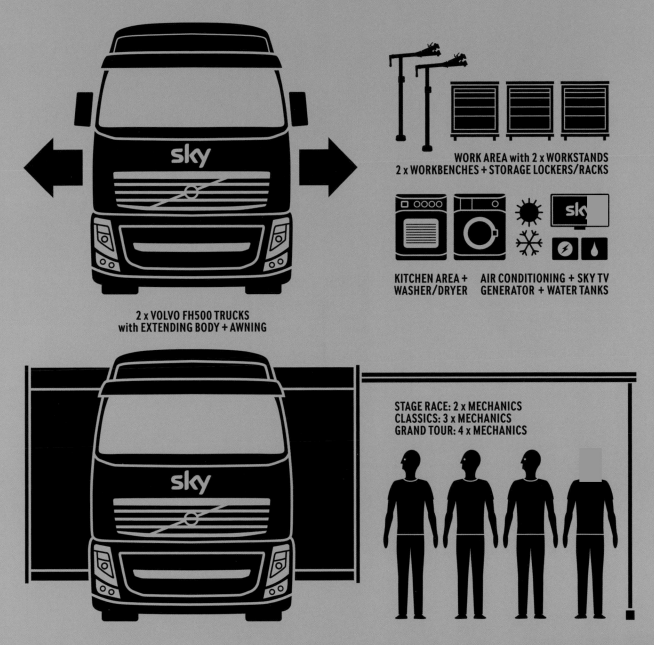

2 x VOLVO FH500 TRUCKS
with EXTENDING BODY + AWNING

WORK AREA with 2 x WORKSTANDS
2 x WORKBENCHES + STORAGE LOCKERS/RACKS

KITCHEN AREA +
WASHER/DRYER

AIR CONDITIONING + SKY TV
GENERATOR + WATER TANKS

STAGE RACE: 2 x MECHANICS
CLASSICS: 3 x MECHANICS
GRAND TOUR: 4 x MECHANICS

SERVICE COURSE – LOTTO BELISOL

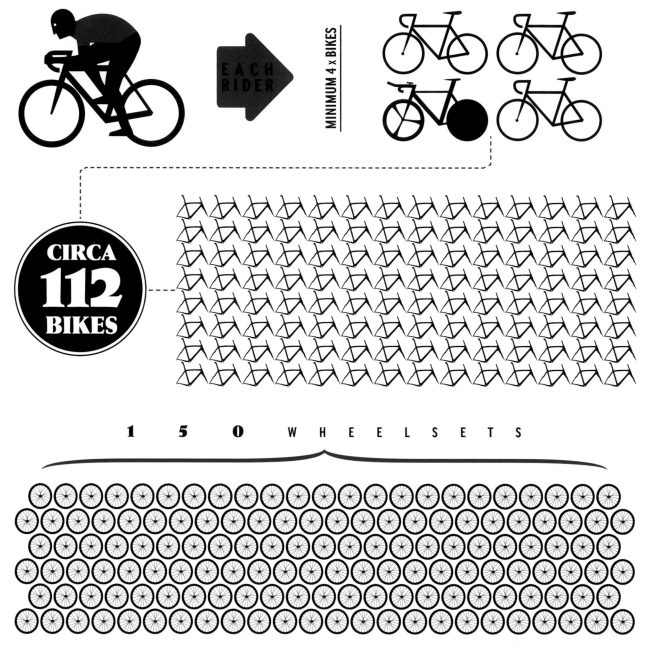

EACH RIDER

MINIMUM 4 x BIKES

CIRCA
112
BIKES

1 5 0 WHEELSETS

ADMINISTRATORS

MECHANICS

KITCHEN TRUCK · SERVICE TRUCK · STORE TRUCK

5 x SERVICE CARS

5 x VIP CARS

BASED NEAR
HERENTALS

ANTWERP
PAAL-BERINGEN

BELGIUM

RIDLEY BIKES

27 RIDERS

DOPING – BLOOD DOPING

EPO

Erythropoietin (EPO) is a naturally occuring hormone produced by bone marrow.

Artificially boosting EPO levels allows the blood to have an increased oxygen carrying capacity through increased red blood cell production.

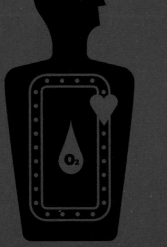

O₂

O₂

EPO was banned by WADA in the early 1990s although a test wasn't available until 2000.

It can cause heart disease, stroke and cerebral or pulmonary embolism due to thickening of the blood.

SYNTHETIC BLOOD SUBSTITUES

Experimental haemoglobin-based oxygen carriers (HBOCs) and chemicals called perfluorocarbons (PFCs) can be added to the bloodstream to increase its oxygen carrying capacity.

Synthetic blood substitutes are banned by WADA and can cause heart-attacks and organ failure.

TRANSFUSIONS

Transfusions may be *autologous* (athlete's own stored blood) or *homologous* (donated blood) and improve performance by increasing the concentration of red blood cells. The technique is banned by WADA despite autologous transfusions being difficult to detect

In addition to the dangers of having thickened blood, risks can also include blood poisoning and organ damage from mis-matched or poorly stored blood.

1 – 4 units of whole blood (1 unit = 450 ml) withdrawn several weeks before competition.

Red blood cells separated from blood plasma and refrigerated or flash-frozen at -80C.

Stored red blood cells reinfused 1 – 7 days before event, increasing oxygen capacity.

DOPING – PERFORMANCE ENHANCING DRUGS (PEDs)

Group of drugs that include the naturally occuring hormone testosterone. Used to artifically promote muscle growth, reduce body fat and reduce recovery time after exercise.

Recently developed drugs that mimic the effects of steroids.

Anabolic steroids have been banned by WADA since the 1980s. Most xenoandrogens are currently legal.

Steroids can cause kidney and liver damage, cardiovascular disease, aggression, infertility and breast growth in men.

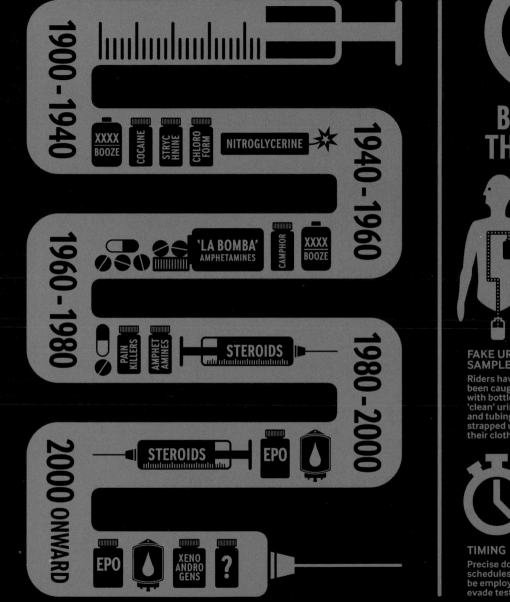

1900 – 1940

1940 – 1960

1960 – 1980

1980 – 2000

2000 ONWARD

XXXX BOOZE

COCAINE

STRYC HNINE

CHLORO FORM

NITROGLYCERINE

'LA BOMBA' AMPHETAMINES

CAMPHOR

XXXX BOOZE

PAIN KILLERS

AMPHET AMINES

STEROIDS

STEROIDS

EPO

EPO

XENO ANDRO GENS

?

BEATING THE TESTS

FAKE URINE SAMPLES

Riders have been caught with bottles of 'clean' urine and tubing strapped under their clothing.

MASKING DRUGS

Masking agents and diuretics hide the presence of PEDs or flush them from the body.

TIMING

Precise doping schedules can be employed to evade testing.

NOVELTY

It can take several years to devise tests for new drugs.

DOPING – LANCE ARMSTRONG & DR FERRARI

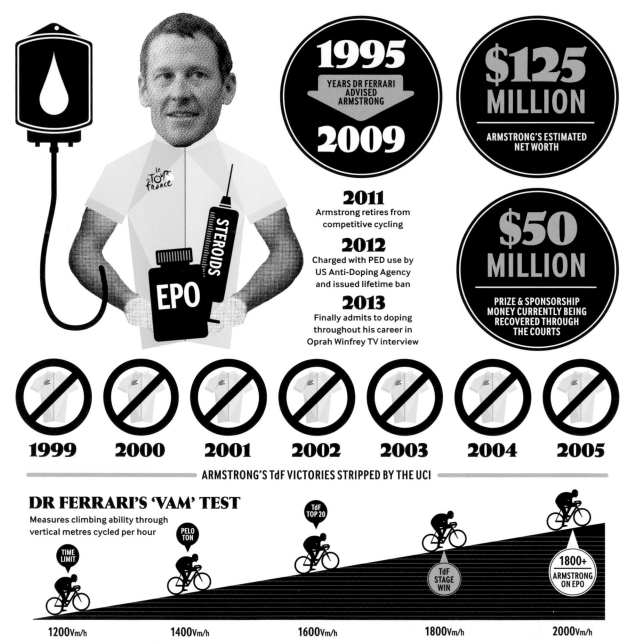

1995

YEARS DR FERRARI ADVISED ARMSTRONG

2009

$125 MILLION

ARMSTRONG'S ESTIMATED NET WORTH

2011
Armstrong retires from competitive cycling

2012
Charged with PED use by US Anti-Doping Agency and issued lifetime ban

2013
Finally admits to doping throughout his career in Oprah Winfrey TV interview

$50 MILLION

PRIZE & SPONSORSHIP MONEY CURRENTLY BEING RECOVERED THROUGH THE COURTS

1999   **2000**   **2001**   **2002**   **2003**   **2004**   **2005**

ARMSTRONG'S TdF VICTORIES STRIPPED BY THE UCI

DR FERRARI'S 'VAM' TEST

Measures climbing ability through vertical metres cycled per hour

TIME LIMIT

PELOTON

TdF TOP 20

TdF STAGE WIN

1800+ ARMSTRONG ON EPO

1200 Vm/h   **1400**Vm/h   **1600**Vm/h   **1800**Vm/h   **2000**Vm/h

S

ONE-DAY CYCLE EVENT
ORGANISED BY ASO - COMPANY THAT STAGES THE TOUR DE FRANCE
MIRRORS A STAGE OF THE TOUR AND SO THE ROUTE CHANGES EACH YEAR

STARTED:
1993

PARDIES-PIÉTAT

ARROS-DE-NAY

NAY

BÉNÉJACO

PONTACO

OSSUN

LANNE

ORINCLES

TREBONS

BAGNÈRES-DE-BIGORRE

ST MARIE-DE-CAMPAIN

2

VILLELONGUE

ARTALENS-SOUIN

F

CHÈZE

LUZ-ST-SAUVEUR

BARÈGES

1

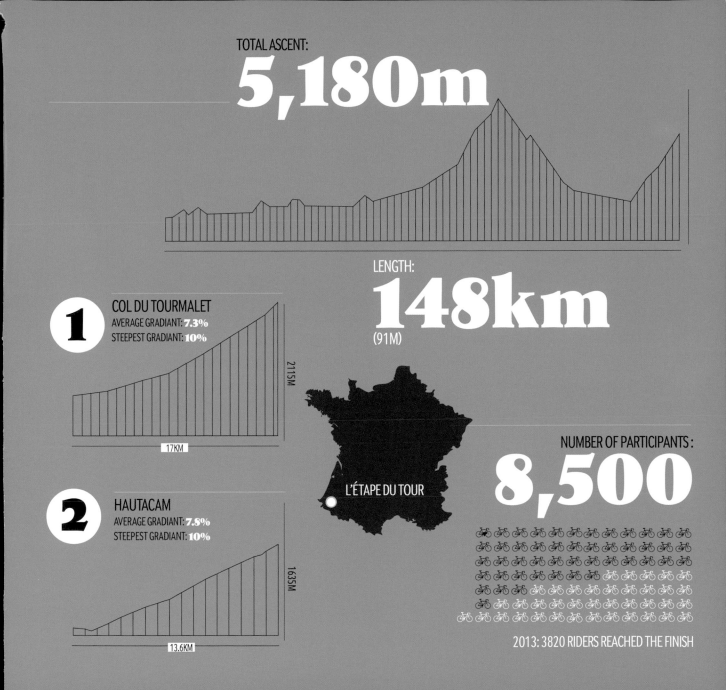

TOTAL ASCENT:
5,180m

LENGTH:
148km
(91M)

NUMBER OF PARTICIPANTS:
8,500

1 COL DU TOURMALET
AVERAGE GRADIANT: **7.3%**
STEEPEST GRADIANT: **10%**

2115M

17KM

2 HAUTACAM
AVERAGE GRADIANT: **7.8%**
STEEPEST GRADIANT: **10%**

1635M

13.6KM

L'ÉTAPE DU TOUR

2013: 3820 RIDERS REACHED THE FINISH

SPORTIVE
LA MARMOTTE

STARTED:
1982

TRANSLATION:
NAMED AFTER LARGE GROUND SQUIRREL COMMON IN THE FRENCH ALPS

LA MARMOTTE

LENGTH:
174.4km
(108.4M)

ONE-DAY RIDE WITH SEVERAL FIRST CATEGORY CLIMBS TO HAVE APPEARED IN THE TOUR DE FRANCE

SAINT-ÉTIENNE DE CUINES
SAINT-ALBAN DES VILLARDS
SAINT-COLOMBAN DES VILLARDS
SAINT-JEAN DE MAURIENNE
SAINT-MICHEL DE MAURIENNE
DÉFILÉ DE MAUPAS
LE RIVIER D'ALLEMOND
LES GRANDES SEIGNÈRES
LE VERNEY
LES VERNEYS
ALLEMONT
LA RIVINE
ROACETAILLEE
GRANGES DU GALIBIEN
BOURG D'OISANS
PLAN LACHAT
LE CLAPIER
LE FRENEY D'OISANS
VILLAR D'ARENE
LA GRAVE

5,180m

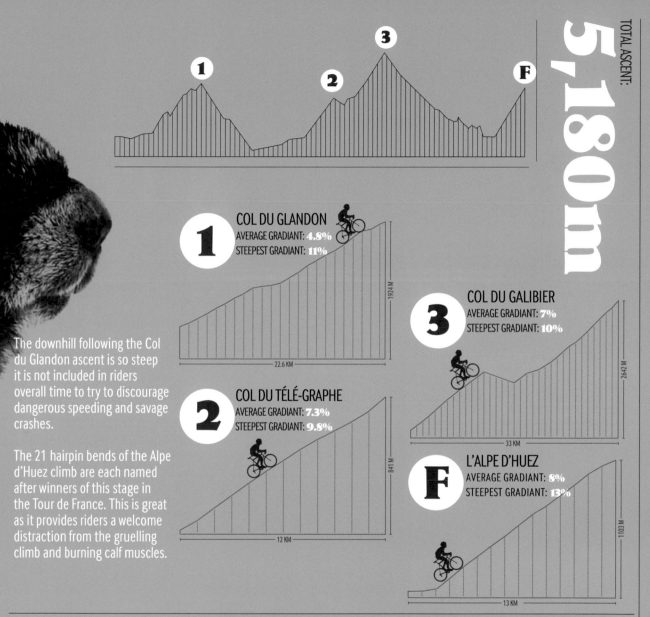

1 COL DU GLANDON
AVERAGE GRADIANT: **4.8%**
STEEPEST GRADIANT: **11%**

1924 M
22.6 KM

3 COL DU GALIBIER
AVERAGE GRADIANT: **7%**
STEEPEST GRADIANT: **10%**

2642 M
33 KM

2 COL DU TÉLÉ-GRAPHE
AVERAGE GRADIANT: **7.3%**
STEEPEST GRADIANT: **9.8%**

841 M
12 KM

F L'ALPE D'HUEZ
AVERAGE GRADIANT: **8%**
STEEPEST GRADIANT: **13%**

1110 M
13 KM

The downhill following the Col du Glandon ascent is so steep it is not included in riders overall time to try to discourage dangerous speeding and savage crashes.

The 21 hairpin bends of the Alpe d'Huez climb are each named after winners of this stage in the Tour de France. This is great as it provides riders a welcome distraction from the gruelling climb and burning calf muscles.

NUMBER OF PARTICIPANTS:

7,000

SPORTIVE
RIDE LONDON-SURREY 100

80'000
PEOPLE ENTRED THE BALLOT
FOR ONLY

25,000
PLACES

STARTED:
2013
FOLLOWING THE MEN'S OLYMPIC ROAD RACE ROUTE FROM LONDON OLYMPIC GAMES 2012

LENGTH:
161km
(100M)

ROADS WILL BE CLOSED ALL ALONG THE ROUTE. LANDMARKS
INCLUDE HARRODS, PARLIAMENT SQUARE, AND WHITEHALL

LONDON-SURREY 100

QUEEN ELIZABETH OLYMPIC PARK

S

F

WATERLOO BRIDGE
LONDON BRIDGE
HYDE PARK CORNER
BLACKFRIARS BRIDGE
THE MALL
HAMMERSMITH
CHISWICK BRIDGE
PUTNEY BRIDGE
TIBBET'S CORNER
HAMPTON COURT BRIDGE
COOMBE LANE
KINGSTON BRIDGE
ESHER COMMON
BYFLEET
OAKLAWN ROAD
RIPLEY
BOX HILL
2
LEITH HILL
1

—— 100 ROUTE
—— CLASSIC ROUTE
〰️ RIVER THAMES

1: The Classic route follows the same roads as the 100 route, with additional loops that the pro riders will follow during the 200km race.

2: At 294m above sea level Leith Hill is the highest point in Surrey. On a clear day you can see 13 counties, the Channel and the London skyline from the top.

203M

1 **2**

SPORTIVE
MARATONA DLES DOLOMITES AKA 'THE MARATONA'

STARTED:
1987

EDITIONS:
28 2014

THE MARATONA

GARDENA PASS
4

SELLA PASS
3

CAMPAGNOLO PASS
1

PORDOI PASS
2

VALPAROLA PASS
5

GIAU PASS
6

LENGTH:
138km
(86M)

THREE COURSES: SELLARONDA, MIDDLE COURSE, IL MARATONA
EACH STARTS IN LA ILA VILLAGE
MARATONA COURSE FINISHES IN CORVARA

CLIMBS: 'THE SELLA GROUP'

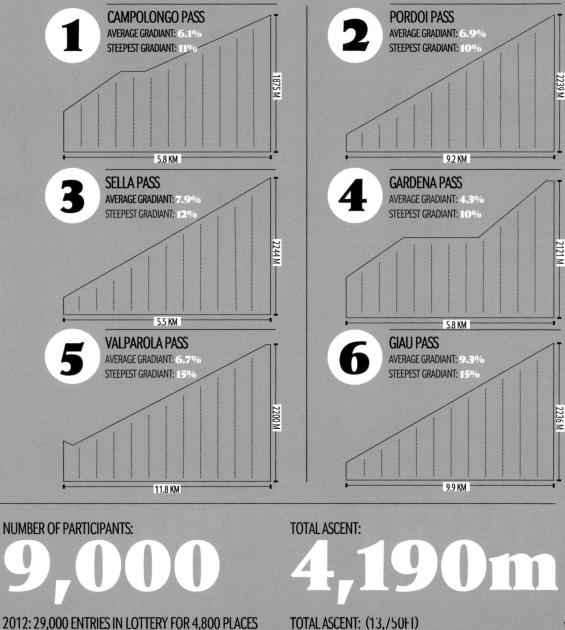

1 CAMPOLONGO PASS
AVERAGE GRADIANT: **6.1%**
STEEPEST GRADIANT: **11%**
1875 M
5.8 KM

2 PORDOI PASS
AVERAGE GRADIANT: **6.9%**
STEEPEST GRADIANT: **10%**
2239 M
9.2 KM

3 SELLA PASS
AVERAGE GRADIANT: **7.9%**
STEEPEST GRADIANT: **12%**
2244 M
5.5 KM

4 GARDENA PASS
AVERAGE GRADIANT: **4.3%**
STEEPEST GRADIANT: **10%**
2121 M
5.8 KM

5 VALPAROLA PASS
AVERAGE GRADIANT: **6.7%**
STEEPEST GRADIANT: **15%**
2200 M
11.8 KM

6 GIAU PASS
AVERAGE GRADIANT: **9.3%**
STEEPEST GRADIANT: **15%**
2236 M
9.9 KM

NUMBER OF PARTICIPANTS:
9,000
2012: 29,000 ENTRIES IN LOTTERY FOR 4,800 PLACES

TOTAL ASCENT:
4,190m
TOTAL ASCENT: (13,750FT)

SPORTIVE
HELL OF THE NORTH

STARTED:
1896 professional race

TRANSLATION:
**Pro road race is known as:
'l'Enfer du Nord' or
'Hell of the North'**

LENGTH:
70/141/170km

EVEN THE LONGEST ROUTE IS CONSIDERABLY SHORTER THAN THE PRO RACE, WHICH IS 258KM
FULL ROUTE, AS RIDDEN BY THE PROS, CONTAINS 28 COBBLED SECTIONS OR 'SECTEURS';
THE COBBLES ARE CALLED PAVÉ

END: ROUBAIX VELODROME

Routes

141 KM
70 KM
170 KM

COBBLED SECTIONS

5 STAR SECTION
CARREFOUR DE L'ARBRE

An opportunity for amateur cyclists to ride the route of the Paris-Roubaix 'Monument Classic' - one of the hardest races in professional cycling.

5 STAR SECTION
TROUÉE D'ARENBERG

L'ENFER DU NORD

The 170km route contains some of the hardest 'secteurs' faced by the pros, including the Trouée d'Arenberg and the Carrefour de l'Arbre.

START: SAINT QUENTIN

CLASSIC CLIMB – ALPE D'HUEZ

FIRST TOUR DE FRANCE
STAGE APPEARANCE

1952

TOTAL NUMBER
OF APPEARANCES

28

ALPE D'HUEZ
BOURG D'OISANS

14%
MAX. GRADIENT

1,143m
▶717m ⌗1,860m
VERTICAL ASCENT

37:35
FASTEST ASCENT
MARCO PANTANI

21
HAIRPIN BENDS
NAMED AFTER
TOUR DE FRANCE
STAGE WINNERS

GIUSEPPE GUERINI ❶
MARCO PANTANI ❷
MARCO PANTANI ❸
ROBERTO CONTI ❹
ANDREW HAMPSTEN ❺
GIANNI BUGNO ❻
GIANNI BUGNO ❼
GERT-JAN THEUNISSE ❽
STEVEN ROOKS ❾
FEDERICO ECHAVE ❿
BERNARD HINAULT ⓫
LUIS HERRERA ⓬
PETER WINNEN ⓭
BEAT BREU ⓮
PETER WINNEN / CHRISTOPHE RIBLON ⓯
JOOP ZOETEMELK / PIERRE ROLLAND ⓰
JOAQUIM AGOSTINO / CARLOS SASTRE ⓱
HENNIE KUIPER / FRANK SCHLECK ⓲
HENNIE KUIPER / LANCE ARMSTRONG ⓳
JOOP ZOETEMELK / IBAN MAYO ⓴
FAUSTO COPPI *(FIRST STAGE WINER 1952)* / ㉑
LANCE ARMSTRONG

DUTCH MOUNTAIN

WINS – **5** WINNERS

JOOP ZOETEMELK

HENNIE KUIPER

PETER WINNEN

GERT-JAN THEUNISSE

STEVEN ROOKS

HAIRPIN 7
DUTCH CORNER

☺ + 🍺 × **1,000s**

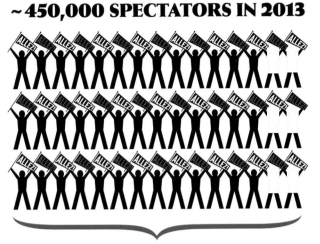

~ **450,000** SPECTATORS IN **2013**

x10,000

REMARKABLE VICTORIES

1984
AMATEUR RIDER LUIS HERRERA BEATS THE
PROFESSIONAL PELOTON WITH SOLO CLIMB

1999
GIUSEPPE GUERINI KNOCKED OFF BY FAN
DURING CLIMB — RECOVERS TO TAKE WIN

1986
BERNARD HINAULT WINS ARM-IN-ARM WITH
GREG LEMOND — A PUBLIC TRUCE AFTER
FALLING OUT EARLIER IN THE RACE

2013
CHRISTOPHE RIBLON WINS AFTER
CLIMBING ALPE D'HUEZ TWICE IN SAME
STAGE — A TOUR DE FRANCE FIRST

CLASSIC CLIMB – MONT VENTOUX

12%
MAX. GRADIENT

1,622m
▶ 287m ▓ 1,909m
VERTICAL ASCENT

MOUNT VENTOUX
BEDOIN

FIRST TOUR DE FRANCE
STAGE APPEARANCE
1951
TOTAL NUMBER
OF APPEARANCES
15

~ · 3.5% · 4.5% · 6% · 6% · 4.5% · 9.5% · 11% · 9% · 10% · 9.5% · 8.5% · 10.5% · 8% · 7.5% · 6% · 7% · 7.5% · 8% · 10%

1 2 3 4 5 6 7 8 9 10 11 12 13 14 15 16 17 18 19 20
— KILOMETRES —

9x SUMMIT FINISHES — **6x** SUMMIT CROSSINGS —

THINGS AT THE TOP

15TH CENTURY CHAPEL

50M RADIO TOWER

METEOROLOGICAL OBSERVATORY

MEMORIAL TO
BRITISH CYCLIST
TOM SIMPSON

EDDIE MERCKX
ON OXYGEN
AFTER 1970 WIN

56+ MPH WIND 240 DAYS A YEAR

55:51
IBAN MAYO
FINISHING A
RECORD ASCENT
2004 CRITERIUM DU
DAUPHINE LIBERE
TIME TRIAL

TOM SIMPSON

COLLAPSED AND DIED ON MOUNT VENTOUX
DURING THE 1967 TOUR DE FRANCE

CLASSIC CLIMB – COL DU TOURMALET

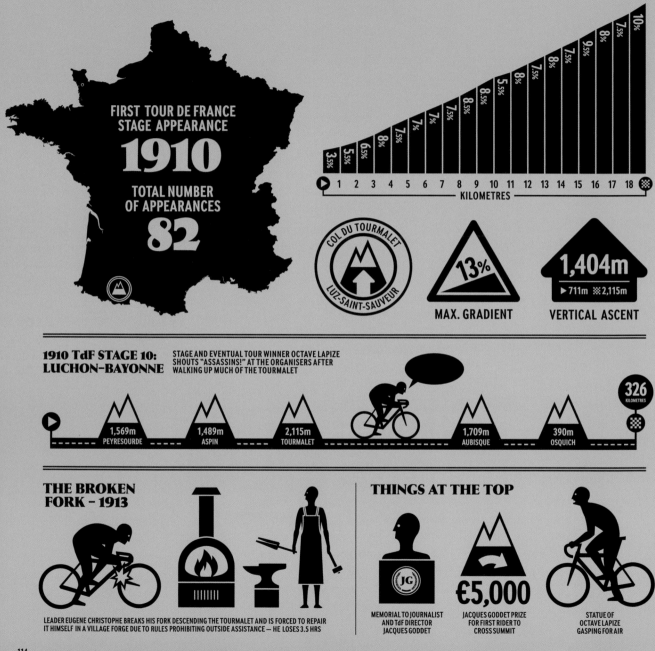

FIRST TOUR DE FRANCE STAGE APPEARANCE

1910

TOTAL NUMBER OF APPEARANCES

82

KILOMETRES

3.5% 5.5% 6.5% 8% 7.5% 7% 7% 7.5% 7.5% 8.5% 8.5% 5.5% 7.5% 8% 7.5% 9.5% 8% 7.5% 10%

1 2 3 4 5 6 7 8 9 10 11 12 13 14 15 16 17 18

COL DU TOURMALET
LUZ-SAINT-SAUVEUR

13%
MAX. GRADIENT

1,404m
▶711m ❀2,115m
VERTICAL ASCENT

1910 TdF STAGE 10: LUCHON-BAYONNE

STAGE AND EVENTUAL TOUR WINNER OCTAVE LAPIZE SHOUTS "ASSASSINS!" AT THE ORGANISERS AFTER WALKING UP MUCH OF THE TOURMALET

326 KILOMETRES

1,569m PEYRESOURDE

1,489m ASPIN

2,115m TOURMALET

1,709m AUBISQUE

390m OSQUICH

THE BROKEN FORK – 1913

LEADER EUGENE CHRISTOPHE BREAKS HIS FORK DESCENDING THE TOURMALET AND IS FORCED TO REPAIR IT HIMSELF IN A VILLAGE FORGE DUE TO RULES PROHIBITING OUTSIDE ASSISTANCE — HE LOSES 3.5 HRS

THINGS AT THE TOP

JG
MEMORIAL TO JOURNALIST AND TdF DIRECTOR JACQUES GODDET

€5,000
JACQUES GODDET PRIZE FOR FIRST RIDER TO CROSS SUMMIT

STATUE OF OCTAVE LAPIZE GASPING FOR AIR

CLASSIC CLIMB – COL D'AUBISQUE

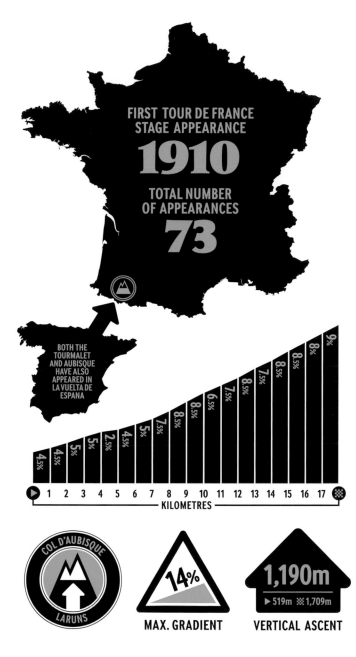

FIRST TOUR DE FRANCE STAGE APPEARANCE

1910

TOTAL NUMBER OF APPEARANCES

73

BOTH THE TOURMALET AND AUBISQUE HAVE ALSO APPEARED IN LA VUELTA DE ESPANA

4.5% 4.5% 5% 5% 2.5% 4.5% 5% 7.5% 8.5% 8.5% 6.5% 7.5% 8.5% 7.5% 8.5% 8.5% 8% 9%

1 2 3 4 5 6 7 8 9 10 11 12 13 14 15 16 17

KILOMETRES

COL D'AUBISQUE

LARUNS

14%

MAX. GRADIENT

1,190m
▶ 519m ※ 1,709m

VERTICAL ASCENT

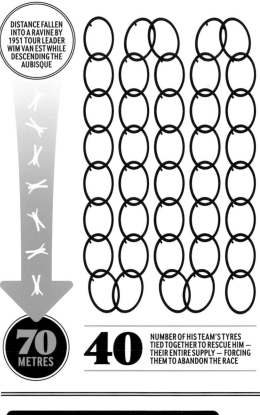

DISTANCE FALLEN INTO A RAVINE BY 1951 TOUR LEADER WIM VAN EST WHILE DESCENDING THE AUBISQUE

70 METRES

40

NUMBER OF HIS TEAM'S TYRES TIED TOGETHER TO RESCUE HIM — THEIR ENTIRE SUPPLY — FORCING THEM TO ABANDON THE RACE

1926 A DOZEN RIDERS SECRETLY FINISH THE STAGE BY BUS

GEAR RATIO NEEDED

39 X **28** to **32**

CLASSIC CLIMB – PASSO STELVIO

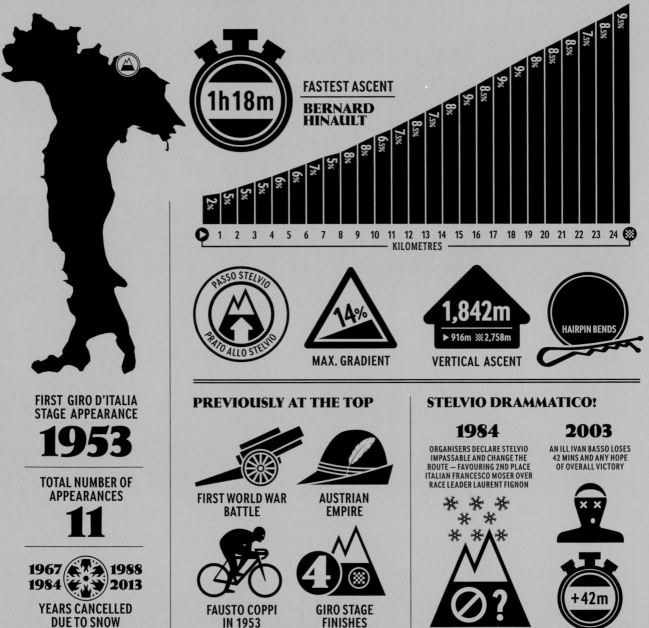

1h18m

FASTEST ASCENT

BERNARD HINAULT

2% 5% 5% 5% 6% 6% 7% 5% 8% 8% 6.5% 7.5% 8.5% 7.5% 8% 9% 8.5% 9% 8% 8.5% 8.5% 7.5% 8.5% 9.5%

▶ 1 2 3 4 5 6 7 8 9 10 11 12 13 14 15 16 17 18 19 20 21 22 23 24 ▦

KILOMETRES

PASSO STELVIO
PRATO ALLO STELVIO

14%

MAX. GRADIENT

1,842m

▶916m ※2,758m

VERTICAL ASCENT

HAIRPIN BENDS

FIRST GIRO D'ITALIA STAGE APPEARANCE

1953

TOTAL NUMBER OF APPEARANCES

11

1967   1988
1984   2013

YEARS CANCELLED DUE TO SNOW

PREVIOUSLY AT THE TOP

FIRST WORLD WAR BATTLE

AUSTRIAN EMPIRE

FAUSTO COPPI IN 1953

4 GIRO STAGE FINISHES

STELVIO DRAMMATICO!

1984

ORGANISERS DECLARE STELVIO IMPASSABLE AND CHANGE THE ROUTE — FAVOURING 2ND PLACE ITALIAN FRANCESCO MOSER OVER RACE LEADER LAURENT FIGNON

2003

AN ILL IVAN BASSO LOSES 42 MINS AND ANY HOPE OF OVERALL VICTORY

Ø?

+42m

CLASSIC CLIMB – MONTE ZONCOLAN

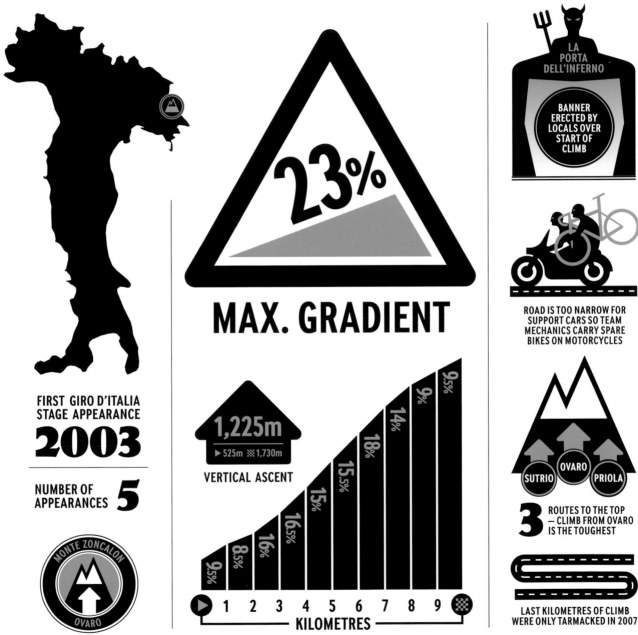

FIRST GIRO D'ITALIA STAGE APPEARANCE
2003

NUMBER OF APPEARANCES **5**

MONTE ZONCALON
OVARO

23%

MAX. GRADIENT

1,225m
▶ 525m ❉ 1,730m
VERTICAL ASCENT

9.5%
8.5%
16%
16.5%
15%
15.5%
18%
14%
9%
9.5%

▶ 1 2 3 4 5 6 7 8 9 🏁
KILOMETRES

LA PORTA DELL'INFERNO
BANNER ERECTED BY LOCALS OVER START OF CLIMB

ROAD IS TOO NARROW FOR SUPPORT CARS SO TEAM MECHANICS CARRY SPARE BIKES ON MOTORCYCLES

SUTRIO OVARO PRIOLA

3 ROUTES TO THE TOP — CLIMB FROM OVARO IS THE TOUGHEST

LAST KILOMETRES OF CLIMB WERE ONLY TARMACKED IN 2007

FIT CLUB – GARMIN

GPS device and website to track athletic performance

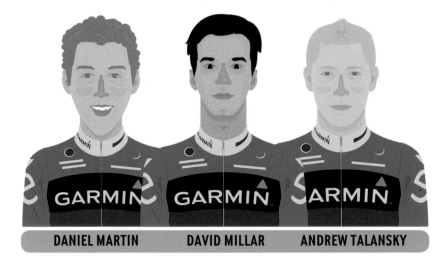

| DANIEL MARTIN | DAVID MILLAR | ANDREW TALANSKY |

Garmin sponsors the Garmin-Sharp UCI WorldTour team.

SATELLITE / GPS   **COMMUNITY**   **SOCIAL**   **FOR CYCLING**

GARMIN CONNECT
Use 'Charts' to display personal performance

Monthly mileage   **Elevation**   **Cadence**

Weather

Call & Text Alerts

Coaching Advice

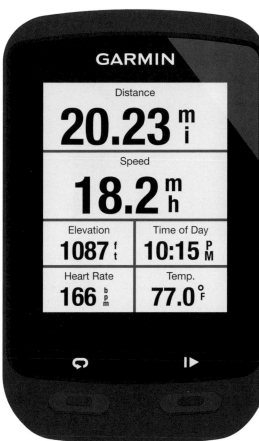

GARMIN

Distance
20.23 mi

Speed
18.2 mh

Elevation	Time of Day
1087 ft	**10:15** PM

Heart Rate	Temp.
166 bpm	**77.0** °F

Garmin Connect

Team Garmin

Traning Plans

Sending/receiving courses and wireless uploads to Garmin Connect.

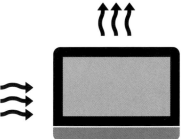

Track from computer at home Round-trip Routing, Route planner training plans connections key destinations.

Integration with compatible Shimano Di2 electronic shifting systems, displays gear selection.

FIT CLUB – STRAVA
Web and mobile app to track athletic performance

LAUNCHED SAN FRANCISCO 2009

COMMUNITY

SATELLITE / GPS

LEADERBOARD
Ranking for times on given segment

FOR CYCLING

FOR RUNNING

KING OF THE MOUNTAINS

The fastest time on a given segment, irrespective of whether it is a climb

SEGMENTS

A section of road 'marked' out on Strava

Segment data includes distance, average gradient, lowest elevation, highest elevation, elevation

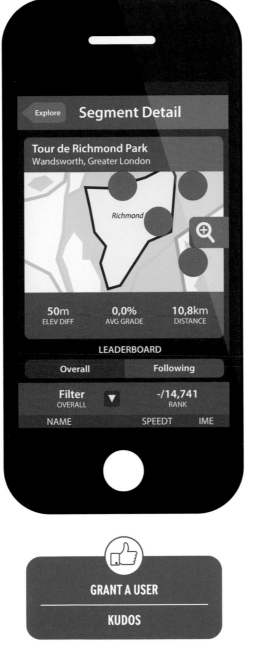

Explore **Segment Detail**

Tour de Richmond Park
Wandsworth, Greater London

Richmond

50m	0,0%	10,8km
ELEV DIFF	AVG GRADE	DISTANCE

LEADERBOARD

Overall	Following

Filter		-/14,741
OVERALL	▼	RANK
NAME	SPEEDT	IME

👍
GRANT A USER
___
KUDOS

MARIANNE VOS

Athlete Profile
Marianne Vos's Activity Last 4 Weeks

PROFESSIONAL RIDERS

Increasing numbers of professional riders publish their ride data on Strava

NIKI TERPSTRA
Published his victorious ride at Paris-Roubaix

Athlete Profile
Niki Terpstra Racing's Activity Last 4 Weeks

POWER TO WEIGHT RATIO (P/KG)

COMMONLY EXPRESSED AS WATTS PER KILO

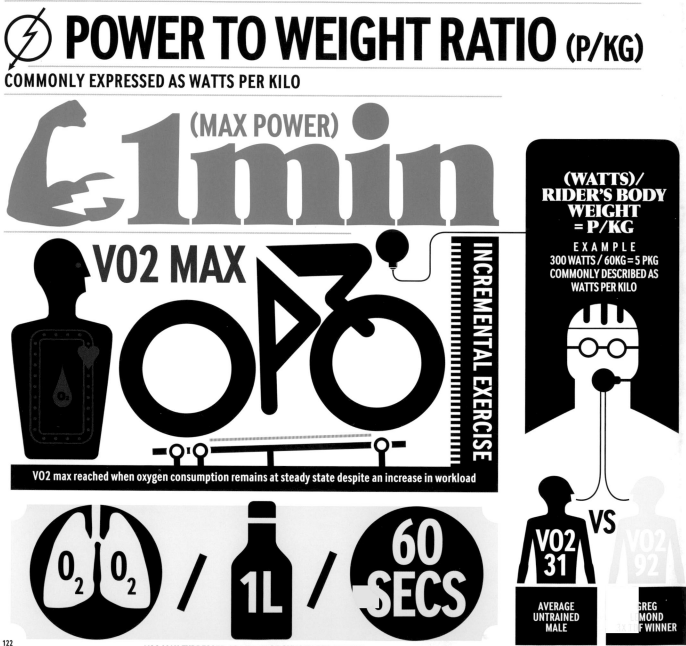

(MAX POWER)
1min

VO2 MAX

INCREMENTAL EXERCISE

VO2 max reached when oxygen consumption remains at steady state despite an increase in workload

(WATTS)/ RIDER'S BODY WEIGHT = P/KG

E X A M P L E
300 WATTS / 60KG = 5 PKG
COMMONLY DESCRIBED AS
WATTS PER KILO

O2 O2 / 1L / 60 SECS

VS

VO2 31

VO2 92

AVERAGE UNTRAINED MALE

GREG LEMOND 3X TDF WINNER

VO2 MAX EXPRESSED AS LITRES OF OXYGEN PER MINUTE

BLOOD TAKEN FROM FINGER DURING EXERCISE AND ANALYSED

VS

FAT

CARBS

DETERMINES HOW MUSCLES USE FUEL MIX

LACTATE THRESHOLD

Level of exercise intensity at which lactate
accumulates in athlete's blood
Determines percentage of VO2 Max
Aerobic capacity that can be used

REFLECTS ABILITY OF MUSCLE TO MATCH ENERGY SUPPLY TO ENERGY DEMAND

⚡ POWER OUTPUT

POWER OUTPUT
measured by a power
meter expressed
in watts

1500 WATTS
MARK CAVENDISH

The best professional
cyclists' sprinting
output

450 WATTS
BRADLEY WIGGINS

The best professional
cyclists' sustained
climbing output

FUNCTIONAL THRESHOLD POWER

60mins

Maximum power that can be sustained for one hour
Expressed in watts
Jealously guarded by professional cyclists

'IT'S OUR COMPETITIVE ADVANTAGE'
Sir Dave Brailsford

TOP SECRET

FIT CLUB – NUMBER CRUNCHERS

⊘VAM
AKA VELOCITÀ ASCENSIONALE MEDIA
VELOCITY, ASCENT, MEAN

VAM = (metres ascended x 60) / Minutes taken to ascend

FINISH

HEIGHT
IN METRES

Average climbing speed - Speed of elevation gain

START

*Phrase coined by Dr Michele Ferrari, Lance Armstrong's trainer

PANTINI VS ARMSTRONG

VOT IZ LE VAM?

TDF 2000

Johan Bruyneel, Armstrong's Team manager, calls Dr Ferrari from the car for an estimate of Pantani's VAM and an assessment of whether he can stay away.

01: Marco Pantani attacks and wins the stage.
02: Lance Armstrong holds back and finishes 4th but retains overall lead.

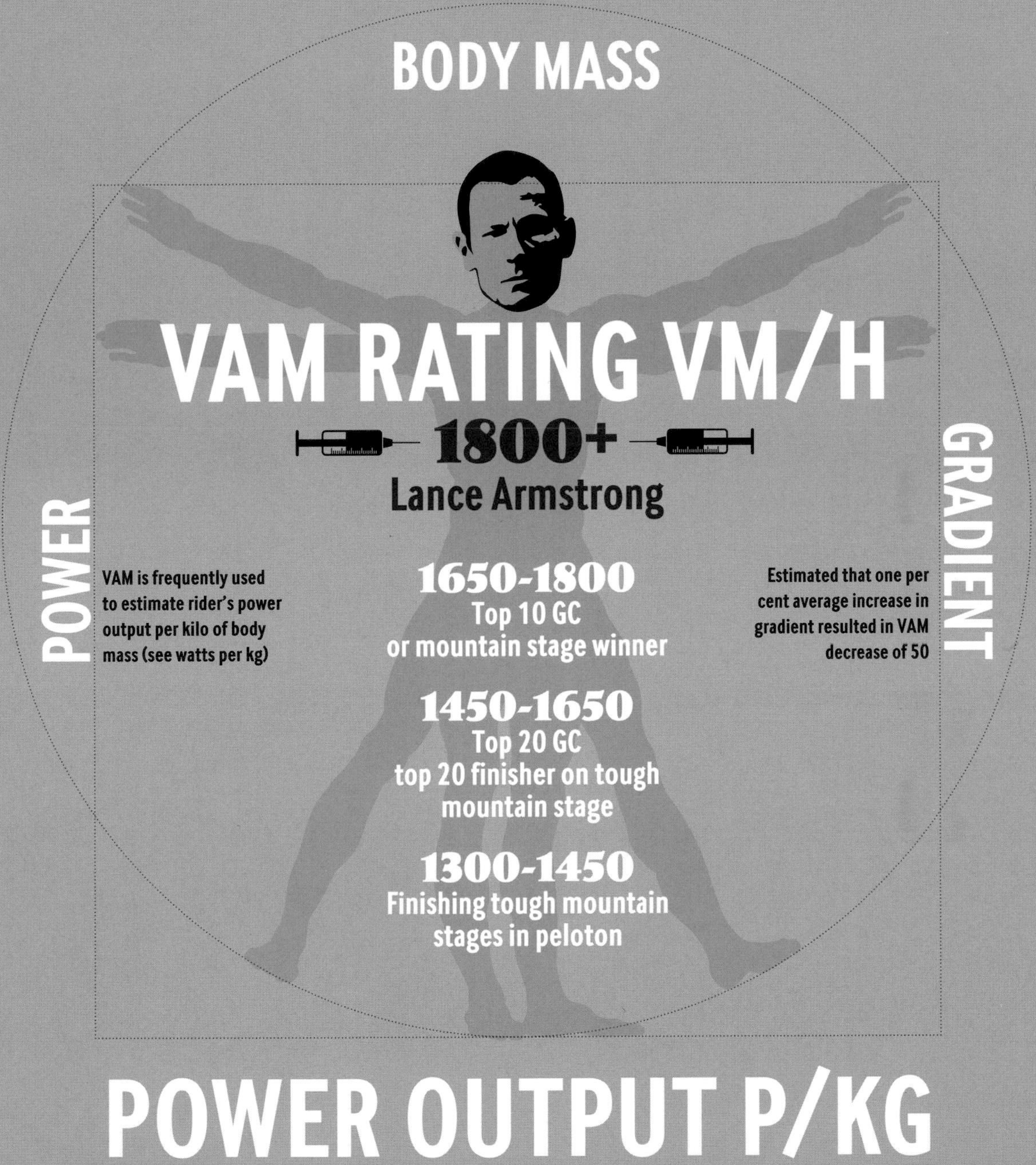

BODY MASS

VAM RATING VM/H

1800+

Lance Armstrong

1650-1800
Top 10 GC
or mountain stage winner

1450-1650
Top 20 GC
top 20 finisher on tough
mountain stage

1300-1450
Finishing tough mountain
stages in peloton

POWER

VAM is frequently used
to estimate rider's power
output per kilo of body
mass (see watts per kg)

GRADIENT

Estimated that one per
cent average increase in
gradient resulted in VAM
decrease of 50

POWER OUTPUT P/KG

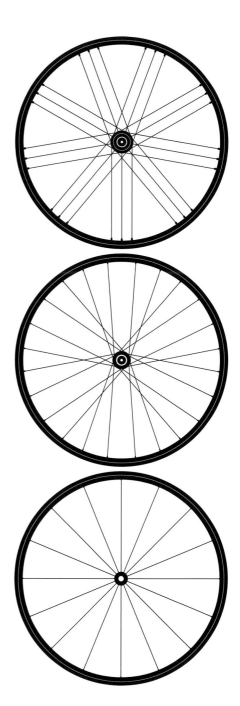

NOTE
While every effort has been made to ensure that the content of this book is as technically accurate and as sound as possible, neither the author nor the publishers can accept responsibility for any injury or loss sustained as a result of the use of this material.

Published by
Bloomsbury Publishing Plc

50 Bedford Square
London WC1B 3DP
www.bloomsbury.com

Bloomsbury is a trademark of
Bloomsbury Publishing Plc

First edition 2014

Copyright © 2014 Road Cycling UK

ISBN (print): 978-1-4729-1054-7
ISBN (ePdf): 978-1-4729-1650-1
ISBN (EPUB): 978-1-4729-1150-6

A CIP catalogue record for this book is available from the British Library.

Acknowledgements

Cover art © Ryan Burisch

Design and illustrations
Matt Ward, Tim Whitlock,
Ryan Burisch, Ryan Van Kesteren,
Micol Montesanti, Thomas Buchinger,
Hattie Scott, Dan Evans, Juste Halavin.

Editor for RoadCyclingUK:
Timothy John

Commissioned by Kirsty Schaper

This book is produced using paper that is made from wood grown in managed, sustainable forests. It is natural, renewable and recyclable. The logging and manufacturing processes conform to the environmental regulations of the country of origin.

Printed and bound in China by
Toppan Leefung Printing

10 9 8 7 6 5 4 3 2 1